Journal of

IRBS

Theological Seminary

**A theological journal committed to
confessional Reformed Baptist theology**

Journal IRBS Theological Seminary (*JIRBSTS*)

Administration

JIRBSTS is administrated for the IRBS board of trustees and edited by:
James M. Renihan, Ph.D., Editor
Richard C. Barcellos, Ph.D., Managing Editor and Book Review Editor
James P. Butler, Associate Editor
Micah Renihan, Associate Editor

Purchasing instructions

JIRBSTS is published on an annual basis. Individual issues can be purchased for $12 USD (plus shipping and handling). If paying by check, make it payable to **RBAP** and write the issue(s) purchasing on the memo line (e.g., *JIRBSTS* 2020). Email rb@rbap.net for orders being paid via check so shipping and handling can be calculated. All back issues are available. Send your check made out to **RBAP** to the following address:

RBAP
c/o Richard Barcellos
349 Sunrise Terrace
Palmdale, CA 93551
On the memo line, please include the issue(s) purchasing.

JIRBSTS may be purchased electronically at www.rbap.net.

Correspondence

General correspondence can be sent to the address above. Email correspondence should be directed to rb@rbap.net.

This journal uses the SBL Greek, SBL Hebrew, and SBL BibLit fonts for biblical languages. More information about the fonts is available at https://www.sbl-site.org/educational/biblicalfonts.aspx.

Published by RBAP, Palmdale, CA
www.rbap.net
Printed in the United States of America.

Cover and formatted for print by Sean Saclolo.

ISBN: 978-0-9965198-7-8

J. GRESHAM MACHEN WAS RIGHT:

Lessons for Southern Baptists

Terry A. Chrisope[*]

Oddly enough for an audience of mostly Baptists, I seek to draw attention to two Presbyterian theologians: J. Gresham Machen (1881–1937) and John H. Leith (1919–2002). The two men had much in common. Both were Southerners: Machen from Maryland, with roots in Virginia and Georgia, Leith from South Carolina. Both were originally connected with the Southern Presbyterian Church (U.S.). Both were highly educated at elite institutions: Machen at Johns Hopkins University, Princeton Theological Seminary, Princeton University, and the German universities of Marburg and Göttingen and Leith at Erskine College, Columbia Theological Seminary, Vanderbilt University, and Yale University. The careers of the two men bookended the twentieth century. Machen was active during the first third of the century and Leith during the last half of the century. Both men were seminary professors: Machen in Greek and NT at Princeton Seminary (1906–29) and Westminster Seminary (1929–36) and Leith in church history at Union Seminary in Richmond, Virginia (1959–90). And both authored books warning of the dangers of theological liberalism.

The title of Machen's book, *Christianity and Liberalism* (1923),[1] sets forth his position at the outset: theological liberalism and Christianity are two different things. Leith's title also announces his stance and sounds something of an alarm, *Crisis in the Church: The Plight of*

---

[*] Terry A. Chrisope is an elder of Legacy Baptist Church of Northwest Arkansas. He was formerly Professor of History and Bible at Missouri Baptist University, and holds the B.A. from Central Baptist College, M.Div. and Th.M. from Covenant Theological Seminary, and Ph.D. from Kansas State University.

Editor's note: Though this article is aimed primarily at Southern Baptists, it is hoped that those outside that communion will both profit from and be warned by this fine contribution to our journal.

[1] J. Gresham Machen, *Christianity and Liberalism* (1923; reprint, Grand Rapids: Wm. B. Eerdmans Publishing Co., 1956).

Theological Education (1997),[2] in which he bemoaned the direction taken by specifically Presbyterian seminaries in the previous several decades. During that time, he argues, they had abandoned their commitment to the historic Christian faith and had fallen into a theological quagmire. In a recent rereading of Leith's book, I was struck by a profound irony—every major issue raised by Leith in 1997 had been addressed by Machen in 1923. My thesis here is twofold: (1) if Presbyterians had heeded Machen's warning in the 1920s, then Leith's book would not have been necessary in 1997 and (2) if Machen was correct in his estimate of the situation, then Southern Baptists in our own day would do well to give heed to Machen's warnings. Southern Baptist history shows we are not immune to the same influences that led to the demise of the once proud Presbyterian church bodies.

John Gresham Machen was a major figure in Reformed and evangelical circles in the early twentieth century. He was born in 1881 to parents possessing a strong Southern heritage, his father in Washington, D.C. and Virginia, his mother from Georgia. His father, Arthur Machen, was a graduate of Harvard Law School, eventually settling into a successful career as a lawyer in Baltimore, Maryland. Machen's mother was Mary (nicknamed "Minnie") Gresham of Macon, Georgia. (According to Machen's biographer, his middle name Gresham [his mother's maiden name] is to be pronounced with a syllable break between the "s" and the "h," with the "h" silent, resulting in no "sh" sound but only Gres-am). J. Gresham was born and grew up in Baltimore. He attended Johns Hopkins University (when it had an undergraduate program) and Princeton Theological Seminary, graduating from the latter in 1905, having shown promise of eminent gifts in scholarship. He studied at the German universities of Marburg and Gottingen in 1905–1906, then returned to teach New Testament Greek at Princeton Seminary, after much hesitation. His hesitation was apparently fostered by an intellectual and spiritual crisis through which he was passing at the time, a crisis not fully resolved until about 1912. He finally saw his way clear to be ordained a Presbyterian minister in 1915, whereupon he was installed as a

---

[2] John H. Leith, *Crisis in the Church: The Plight of Theological Education* (Louisville: Westminster John Knox Press, 1997).

regular faculty member of Princeton Seminary, where he served until 1929. Machen lived during the ascendancy of theological liberalism or "modernism" in the northern Christian denominations; it gained control of most of them in the 1920s, including the Northern Presbyterian Church (U.S.A.). During that decade, Machen published several books, including *The Origin of Paul's Religion* (1921), *New Testament Greek for Beginners* (1923), *Christianity and Liberalism* (1923), *What Is Faith* (1925), and *The Virgin Birth of Christ* (1930). When Princeton Seminary was reorganized on a more liberal basis in 1929, Machen departed to found Westminster Theological Seminary in Philadelphia. In the early 1930s, Machen participated in the Independent Board for Presbyterian Foreign Missions, not wanting to contribute funds to support the liberal mission efforts of the Presbyterian Church, USA (Northern). Upon the demand of the denomination that he terminate his relationship with the board, he refused, whereupon he was tried (without being allowed a defense), convicted, and defrocked (suspended from the ministry) in 1935. Thereafter Machen was instrumental in forming the denomination that became the Orthodox Presbyterian Church. Wearing himself out in pursuance of his many academic and ecclesiastical responsibilities, he died of pneumonia on January 1, 1937, while ministering in North Dakota.[3]

Machen's intellectual and spiritual struggle from 1905 to 1915 was severe and profoundly affected the rest of his life and career.[4] It left him convinced that Christianity and theological liberalism constituted two different religions, a conclusion which lay at the bottom of his later public stance as well as of his scholarly and popular writings. John Leith had come to a similar conclusion by the end of his career, but tragically by then it was too late for Leith's warning to have much practical effect. Leith's denomination, the Southern Presbyterian Church (U.S.), which had previously tended to remain more

---

[3] The major and standard treatment of Machen's life is Ned B. Stonehouse, *J. Gresham Machen: A Biographical Memoir* (Grand Rapids: Eerdmans, 1955). For a more recent biography, see D. G. Hart, *Defending the Faith: J. Gresham Machen and the Crisis of Conservative Protestantism in Modern America* (Grand Rapids: Baker Books, 1995).

[4] For a study of Machen's intellectual crisis and its aftermath, see Terry A. Chrisope, *Toward a Sure Faith: J. Gresham Machen and the Dilemma of Biblical Criticism, 1881–1915* (Fearn, Ross-shire, U.K.: Christian Focus Publications, 2000).

conservative than the northern body, had already joined with that more liberal denomination in 1983 to become part of the Presbyterian Church (USA). Leith pointed out several areas of concern in his book of 1997, all of which Machen had identified by 1923 or earlier: (1) liberalism's abandonment of Christianity's historical and doctrinal core; (2) liberalism's grounding in an anti-Christian intellectual foundation; (3) liberalism's difference from Christianity at every essential point of doctrine; (4) liberalism's dishonesty in undermining historic Christianity from within professedly Christian institutions; and (5) liberalism's distortion of Christianity by the introduction of various agendas for radical social transformation as advocated by pressure groups within the church. These five areas of concern will be considered as earlier addressed by Machen.

Christianity Is Historical and Doctrinal

Machen never seemed to tire of asserting that biblical Christianity is characterized by two features: in its essence it is both historical and doctrinal.

1. Christianity is historical

Machen vigorously affirmed that the gospel which is at the basis of Christianity is essentially a narration of historical events. Christianity, he insisted, was based on an account of events involving Jesus Christ and occurring in the space-time history of this world. He wrote, "The primitive Church was concerned . . . primarily, with what Jesus had done. The world was to be redeemed through the proclamation of an event."[5] Biblical Christianity is necessarily connected to history; this fact helps us understand the meaning of the term "gospel." Elsewhere Machen affirmed:

> Give up history, and you can retain some things. You can retain belief in God. . . . You can retain a lofty ethical ideal. But be perfectly clear about one point—you can never retain a gospel. For gospel means "good news," tidings, information about something that has

---

[5] Machen, *Christianity and Liberalism*, 29.

happened. In other words, it means history. A gospel independent of history is simply a contradiction in terms.[6]

Machen seems to accurately reflect the emphasis of the NT. There is no Christianity apart from the redemptive events described in the NT, for Christianity is founded on those events. It is not founded on a set of ideas, on eternal spiritual principles, on religious philosophy, or on a system of ethical teaching, but on something that happened in history. The gospel, Machen maintained, is an account of something that happened — it is "good news."

Keeping this fact before us will keep us from taking many a wrong turn. If we would be faithful in proclaiming the biblical gospel, we must recognize that before all else comes history. The Bible records many events in the history of redemption, but all of them point to, find their center in, and flow out of the events involving Jesus Christ — his incarnation, life, death, resurrection, and exaltation. These events are at the heart of the gospel, those which heralds of the gospel ought to be announcing. They were brought about by a power from outside this world, from outside the natural order — from outside this universe, in fact, yet active within it. This is the power of the infinite, personal, and holy God who is creator, sustainer, and ruler of all. History, in the form of supernaturally wrought events, is fundamental to the biblical gospel.

2. Christianity is doctrinal

Not only is history essential, so is doctrine, for doctrine explains the meaning of the historical events. Completing the assertion cited above concerning the Christian proclamation, Machen wrote, "And with that event went the meaning of the events; and the setting forth of the event with the meaning of the event was doctrine. The narration of the facts is history; the narration of the facts with the meaning is doctrine."[7] With a bit more fulness, Machen put it this way:

---

[6] J. Gresham Machen, "History and Faith" in *What Is Christianity? and Other Addresses*, ed. Ned B. Stonehouse (Grand Rapids: Wm. B. Eerdmans Publishing Co., 1951), 171.

[7] Machen, *Christianity and Liberalism*, 29.

From the beginning, the Christian gospel, as indeed the name 'gospel' or 'good news' implies, consisted in an account of something that had happened. And from the beginning, the meaning of the happening was set forth; and when the meaning of the happening was set forth, then there was Christian doctrine. 'Christ died' – that is history; 'Christ died for our sins' – that is doctrine. Without these two elements, joined in an absolutely indissoluble union, there is no Christianity.[8]

Doctrine tells us the meaning of the events of Jesus' incarnation, death, and resurrection: namely that Jesus Christ is the agent of God's revelation, redemption, and rule – that through him alone God has fully disclosed himself; that through him God accomplished redemption of fallen humans and reconciles them to himself; that through him God is ruling the universe, and now commands all people everywhere to bow the knee to him. Put in a different way, doctrine could be said to constitute the intellectual content of Christianity. These teachings are the assertions that Christianity affirms to be true. Doctrine states the content of the belief system which Christianity affirms, to which it adheres, and which it proclaims.[9]

If we Christians are not proclaiming these events along with their interpretation as provided by the NT, then we are not proclaiming the biblical gospel. Events recorded equal history; events plus their meaning equal doctrine. History and doctrine together equal the gospel. At times in the past, some Southern Baptists have seemed indifferent to history and allergic to doctrine. It should not be so; we should delight in these truths and glory in the proclamation of them. This should be why we stand in the pulpit every Sunday.

Liberalism Incorporates an Anti-Supernaturalistic Bias

At the very beginning of *Christianity and Liberalism* Machen identified the primary intellectual assumption of liberalism, an outlook which

---

[8] Machen, *Christianity and Liberalism*, 27.

[9] By the end of his life, Leith found it necessary to overcome his fear of "oppressive orthodoxy" and to specify what he called "foundational doctrines" which are essential to historic Christianity. See Leith, *Crisis in the Church*, 29–33.

we could call "naturalistic historicism." This outlook involved two components, the first of which was naturalism, which Machen found to be the common factor amidst the varying forms which liberal theology took. He wrote, "the many varieties of modern liberal religion are rooted in naturalism—that is, in the denial of any entrance of the creative power of God . . . in connection with the origin of Christianity."[10] According to a current standard dictionary, the philosophy of naturalism is "the belief that the natural world, as explained by scientific laws, is all that exists and that there is no supernatural or spiritual creation, control, or significance."[11] Naturalism is the teaching that nothing exists except nature, the natural cosmos, and that is all. There is no God who is creator and ruler of the universe whose being transcends the physical universe but who also acts within it. Theological liberalism could not adopt a strict atheistic naturalism because liberalism professed to be Christian, but it is pushed toward a religious naturalism by its emphasis on the immanence of God, the idea that God is present in and through the natural order and does not act independently of it. On this footing, religion must be based on that which naturally occurs in the world, not on a direct act of God.

The second component of the liberal outlook is "historicism," a set of assumptions about history. Historian Grant Wacker defines this stance as "a philosophical orientation" incorporating "three closely related assumptions about the relation between history and knowledge."[12] These assumptions could be termed the developmental, the epistemological, and the explanatory assumptions; they presume that all the events and cultural products of human history have originated, may be known, and must be explained as the result of a process of ceaseless change involving natural historical factors alone. The outlook of historicism was aptly described by Machen in his inaugural address upon being inducted into the regular faculty of Princeton Seminary in 1915: "The world, it

---

[10] Machen, *Christianity and Liberalism*, 2.

[11] *Webster's New World College Dictionary*, 4th ed. (Foster City, CA: IDG Books, 2001), 960.

[12] Grant Wacker, *Augustus H. Strong and the Dilemma of Historical Consciousness* (Macon, GA: Mercer University Press, 1985), 16.

is said, must be explained as an absolutely unbroken development, obeying fixed laws."[13] All three of the assumptions of historicism are fairly well summarized in this single sentence ("development," "must," "explained"). Given these assumptions, the outcome for Christianity is clear: Jesus was not a supernatural person, the Bible is not a supernatural book, and no supernatural events occurred in the origin of Christianity. An infinite-personal transcendent God was not active in these events, which accordingly could not have occurred the way they are described in the NT. Every apparently supernatural occurrence in the Bible must be understood and explained instead as the product of natural historical forces and ordinary human factors.

We need to be aware that these assumptions came to prevail in the modern approach to the Bible, known as the historical-critical method. Take, for example, Rudolf Bultmann (b. 1884), a younger contemporary of Machen, by general agreement the most influential NT scholar of the twentieth century. Bultmann defined the "historical method" as including

> the presupposition that history is a unity in the sense of a closed continuum of effects in which individual events are connected by the succession of cause and effect. . . . This closedness means that the continuum of historical happenings cannot be rent by the interference of supernatural, transcendent powers. . . .[14]

If this is not an explicit atheism, it is at least a functional or methodological atheism, for it decrees that the activity of a transcendent God cannot be allowed to account for any of the historical events in the origin of the Christian movement. Philosopher William J. Abraham has observed, "in the modern period of biblical studies the drive to read the text as functional atheists was very powerful."[15] He continues, "the general reality has been that Scripture

---

[13] Machen, "History and Faith," 175.

[14] Cited in Chrisope, *Toward a Sure Faith,* 211, n. 25.

[15] William J. Abraham, "Scripture and Christian Theology," in David Lyle Jeffrey and C. Stephen Evans, eds., *The Bible and the University,* Scripture and Hermeneutics Series, vol. 8 (Grand Rapids: Zondervan, 2007), 40–57, citations from 44. Abraham goes on to observe that the postmodern era has reached the point of denying a given and stable meaning in a text, including the biblical text, 44–45. This does not mean,

scholars methodologically have had to describe and explain the phenomena of the text as if God does not exist."[16] This approach, when applied, is deadly to genuine Christian faith, eliminating the supra-natural activity of God and thus undermining confidence in the truthfulness and authority of the Bible and the historicity of the events it portrays. This viewpoint exercised considerable influence at Southern Baptist colleges and seminaries over several decades; only the conservative resurgence beginning in 1979 brought a course-reversal at the seminaries (one need only read Greg Wills's recent history of Southern Seminary to verify this[17]). As Machen argued, "You cannot . . . be indifferent to Bible criticism. Let us not deceive ourselves. The Bible is at the foundation of the Church. Undermine that foundation, and the Church will fall."[18] Perpetual vigilance is required to keep naturalistic historicism from exercising its pernicious influence.[19]

Those who are affiliated with the Southern Baptist Founders Conference may perhaps take a measure of encouragement from the fact that our Reformed theology is, in its essence, the very antithesis of naturalism. Princeton theologian B. B. Warfield, a teacher and colleague of Machen, famously argued that Calvinism is simply biblical supernaturalism come into its own. From foreordination, to creation, through the order of salvation, all is acknowledged to be from God, through God, and unto God. It seems likely that only a thoroughgoing Calvinism will survive as the sole alternative ideology to remain standing as our society falls into the abyss of the worship of the creature (i.e., of humanity); everything else will collapse. Yet we cannot be complacent. As 1 Peter 5:8-9 warns, "Your adversary the devil prowls around like a roaring lion, seeking someone to devour. Resist him, firm in your faith." Both Machen and Leith belonged to

---

however, that the anti-supernaturalistic bias has disappeared from the postmodern academy.

[16] Abraham, "Scripture and Christian Theology," 44.

[17] Gregory A. Wills, *Southern Baptist Theological Seminary, 1859–2009* (New York: Oxford University Press, 2009), especially chapters 6 through 12.

[18] Machen, "History and Faith," 183–84.

[19] Leith also mentioned this central element of theological liberalism, referring to it as "Troeltschian historicism." See Leith, *Crisis in the Church*, 36.

confessedly Reformed denominations, yet both groups fell into unbelief—highlighting the need for constant alertness.

Theological Liberalism Is Non-Christian in Nature

Theological liberalism was a movement to reconceptualize Christianity in an effort to make it more amenable to modern thought and sensibility. In short, it sought to "redefine or modify traditional doctrines."[20] Machen argued that liberalism had so revised the doctrinal content of historic Christianity that it ceased to be Christian. It constituted a different belief system, a different religion.

1. Liberalism acknowledges a different source of authority.

"Christianity," Machen wrote, "is founded on the Bible. It bases on the Bible both its thinking and its life. Liberalism, on the other hand is founded upon the shifting emotions of sinful men."[21] For theological liberalism, following the teaching of German theologian Friedrich Schleiermacher, the authority is that of individual, personal experience. Machen observed, "The real authority, for liberalism, can only be 'the Christian consciousness,' or 'Christian experience,'" which at bottom amounts to "individual experience." That, he said, is "no authority at all," for no absolute truth is involved,[22] only the autonomous individual. Today we are seeing where such subjectivism leads—to the claim of absolute personal autonomy.

2. Liberalism adheres to a different belief system in its content.

Along with this shift in authority goes a profound difference in intellectual content. Machen demonstrated that religious liberalism departed from historic Christian teaching at every significant point. In

---

[20] Millard J. Erickson, *Concise Dictionary of Christian Theology* (Grand Rapids: Baker Book House, 1986), 96.

[21] Machen, *Christianity and Liberalism*, 79.

[22] Machen, *Christianity and Liberalism*, 78.

most cases, the substitute beliefs betray the naturalistic roots of liberalism.[23]

Concerning God, Machen held that Christianity adheres to rational theism, acknowledging God as both transcendent and personal, the spiritual Father of those who are in Christ by faith. Liberalism, in contrast, adheres to a purely immanent deity either dwelling within nature ("the mighty world process,") or identical with nature (pantheism; "even when it is not consistently pantheistic, [it] is at any rate pantheizing"),[24] and the Father of all humans without distinction. The result is that liberalism "tends everywhere to break down the separateness between God and the world, and the sharp personal distinction between God and man"; it loses "the awful transcendence of God."[25] The incarnation is often viewed as a symbol of the oneness of humanity with God.

Man, in the Christian view, is considered a sinner who is under the just condemnation of God. The liberal view of man is characterized by a loss of the consciousness of sin and by a confidence in the goodness of man. Machen compared liberalism to naturalistic paganism. "Paganism is optimistic with regard to unaided human nature . . . Christianity is the religion of the broken heart."[26]

Christianity sees Jesus as the object of faith, the divinely-appointed means of dealing with sin through his redeeming work and subsequent human trust in him. For liberalism, Jesus is merely the example of faith. This difference "depends upon a profound difference as to the question who Jesus was." Machen argued that "liberalism regards Jesus as the fairest flower of humanity," but a mere man nevertheless; "Christianity regards Him as a supernatural Person."[27] For Christianity, "Jesus was no mere man but the eternal Son of God."[28]

---

[23] Machen's description of the beliefs of liberalism is general but accurate, as can be substantiated by comparing it with the treatment in John Dillenberger and Claude Welch, *Protestant Christianity Interpreted Through Its Development*, 2nd ed. (New York: Macmillan Publishing Co., 1988), 194–200.

[24] Machen, *Christianity and Liberalism*, 63.

[25] Machen, *Christianity and Liberalism*, 63, 62.

[26] Machen, *Christianity and Liberalism*, 65.

[27] Machen, *Christianity and Liberalism*, 96.

[28] Machen, *Christianity and Liberalism*, 126.

Salvation in liberalism becomes something less than that described in the NT. "Liberalism finds salvation in man"[29]; "the world's evil may be overcome by the world's good; no help is thought to be needed from outside the world."[30] In theological liberalism, "religion itself, and even God, are made merely a means for the betterment of conditions upon this earth,"[31] useful for solving the social problems that afflict the world. The Christian view finds salvation "in an act of God" by which he reconciles humans to himself.[32] Machen describes the supernatural actions of God in providing atonement for sin through the death of Christ and applying it to humans in the new birth, justification, and sanctification.[33]

The church, for liberalism, becomes an agency for social transformation. The practical expression of theological liberalism was a movement known as "the social gospel," a term which Machen used at times.[34] Its aim was to solve the social problems of the modern world. For Machen, genuinely Christian churches were made up of people who had been redeemed; their aim was to proclaim the gospel of redemption from sin through Christ, and then "the true transformation of society will come by the influence of those who have themselves been redeemed."[35]

3. Liberalism is a different religion than historic Christianity.

The affirmation that liberalism is a distinct religion from Christianity is the central argument of *Christianity and Liberalism*, as reflected in its title. In the Introduction, Machen stated his thesis clearly: "we shall be interested in showing that despite the liberal use of traditional phraseology modern liberalism not only is a different religion from Christianity but belongs in a totally different class of religions."[36] The basis of this critique was that liberalism had emptied the Christian

---

[29] Machen, *Christianity and Liberalism*, 117.
[30] Machen, *Christianity and Liberalism*, 136.
[31] Machen, *Christianity and Liberalism*, 149.
[32] Machen, *Christianity and Liberalism*, 117.
[33] See Machen, *Christianity and Liberalism*, 136–48.
[34] Machen, *Christianity and Liberalism*, 152.
[35] Machen, *Christianity and Liberalism*, 158.
[36] Machen, *Christianity and Liberalism*, 7.

faith of its original intellectual content. He argued, "the liberal attempt at reconciling Christianity with modern science has really relinquished everything distinctive of Christianity."[37] What emerges is a religion very much unlike that faith which is found in the NT.[38]

Early in the book, Machen acknowledged that there were different forms of theological liberalism.[39] But near the end of the book, he argued vigorously that liberalism

> is no mere heresy—no mere divergence at isolated points from Christian teaching. On the contrary it proceeds from a totally different root, and it constitutes, in essentials, a unitary system of its own. That does not mean that all liberals hold all parts of the system, or that   Christians who have been affected by liberal teaching at one point have been affected at all points. . . . But the true way in which to examine a spiritual movement is in its logical relations; logic is the great dynamic, and the logical implications of any way of thinking are sooner or later certain to be worked out.[40]

That being the case, the internal logic of the system will prevail. Liberalism "is tending more and more to eliminate from itself illogical remnants of Christian belief"[41] It casts off those elements of traditional Christian belief that do not fit within its system. Machen warned, "the present situation must not be ignored but faced. Christianity is being attacked from within by a movement which is anti-Christian to the core."[42]

By way of application, it seems that it would fall upon us who profess to adhere to biblical Christianity to be faithful in declaring "the whole counsel of God" (Acts 20:27) as found in Scripture, but especially two core doctrines—the character of God and the nature of

---

[37] Machen, *Christianity and Liberalism*, 7.

[38] Leith also came to this realization. In modern theology, in *Crisis in the Church*, 31, he said, "Skepticism about history or the Gospel presentation of Jesus Christ has replaced skepticism about experience. This reversal undermines classical Christianity and replaces it with *a new religion* that survives only by using old Christian words." Emphasis added.

[39] Machen, *Christianity and Liberalism*, 2.

[40] Machen, *Christianity and Liberalism*, 172–73.

[41] Machen, *Christianity and Liberalism*, 173.

[42] Machen, *Christianity and Liberalism*, 173.

Christ's atonement. First, we must proclaim a God who is infinite, personal, and holy. The God of the Bible is One whose being transcends this universe and whose existence is independent of it, a transcendent and sovereign God, the self-existent and infinite creator, sustainer, and ruler of this world, able to act in its affairs. This God is also a personal being (indeed a Trinity of persons) who designed his personal creatures (humans) for relationship with himself in which they acknowledge and honor him. Furthermore, this God is holy, possessing absolute moral purity and the majesty of unique excellence, and who will hold his personal creatures accountable for their thoughts, words, and deeds. With such a conception of God in place, the biblical story is no longer necessarily rendered metaphysically impossible or historically unbelievable.

Second, because of what may be called the "logic of liberalism," another doctrine which we must maintain with the greatest care is that of the substitutionary atonement accomplished by Jesus Christ in his death. As Machen pointed out, the logical implications of any position will eventually work themselves out. If Christ did not die as a propitiatory sacrifice for human sinners, then it follows that they do not logically need a divine-human Savior to offer such a perfect atonement; as a result, the doctrine of the deity of Christ becomes unnecessary and will ultimately be lost. If the deity of Christ is lost, then the idea of a true incarnation is lost as well, in consequence of which the entire edifice of historic Christian faith collapses. The atonement is a keystone of that edifice.[43]

We may acknowledge that the theological situation has changed since Machen's critique of liberalism, especially with the rise of neo-orthodoxy, often considered a reaction against liberalism. Nevertheless, neo-orthodoxy has retained crucial elements of liberalism: (1) the historicist approach to the Bible with its assumptions; (2) the resulting distancing itself from history; and (3) its consequent subjectivism. While many of the specific doctrinal formulations changed in neo-orthodoxy, yet the theological

---

[43] I have argued this case at length in "An Audacious Proposal: The Doctrine of the Atonement and Its Place in Maintaining the Integrity of Christian Higher Education," *Integrite: A Faith and Learning Journal* 13, no. 2 (Fall 2014): 3–22. This journal is published by Missouri Baptist University, St. Louis.

underpinnings of liberalism have not been repudiated, and much of Machen's critique is still valid.[44]

Liberalism Is Dishonest in Promoting its Views under the Guise and Auspices of Christianity

Machen maintained that theological liberals were guilty of rank dishonesty and a failure of integrity in at least two ways.

1. Liberals were dishonest in appropriating traditional biblical language.

Three times in *Christianity and Liberalism* Machen indicted theological liberals for their lack of integrity. Early on, he criticized liberal teachers in colleges and seminaries who disclosed to students their "advanced" views while hiding those views from people in the churches in order to "avoid giving offense."[45] This, Machen said, comes "perilously near dishonesty; the religious teacher, in his heart of hearts, is well aware of the radicalism of his views, but is unwilling to relinquish his place in the hallowed atmosphere of the Church by speaking his whole mind."[46] Later Machen contrasted the views about Jesus Christ of evangelicals and liberals and suggested, "It is high time that this issue should be faced; it is high time that the misleading use of traditional phrases should be abandoned and men should speak their full mind."[47] The problem, Machen charged, was that

> the liberals resort constantly to a double use of language. . . . [H]e attaches to the words a different meaning from that which is attached to them by the simple-minded person to whom he is

---

[44] Quite early among American evangelicals, Machen had read neo-orthodox theologian Karl Barth and offered a critique as early as 1928. See Terry A. Chrisope, "J. Gresham Machen on Barthianism," *The Banner of Truth*, Issue 330 (March 1991) 17–21.

[45] Such language, echoing that of some liberals, was utilized by Machen in *Christianity and Liberalism*, 17, and according to Wills, was the language and tactic used by the theological "progressives" among Southern Baptists during this era. See *Southern Baptist Theological Seminary*, 273–75.

[46] Machen, *Christianity and Liberalism*, 17–18.

[47] Machen, *Christianity and Liberalism*, 109.

speaking. He offends, therefore, against the fundamental principle of truthfulness in language.[48]

Finally, in the last chapter of the book, entitled "The Church," Machen offered an extended, ten-page treatment of the matter. The heart of his argument is that "evangelical churches are creedal churches, and that if a man does not accept their creed he has no right to a place in their teaching ministry."[49] Machen used the ordination vows of the Presbyterian church as an illustration. Men pledge that they believe in the Bible as the infallible word of God, and that they receive and adopt the Westminster Confession "as containing the system of doctrine taught in the Holy Scriptures," yet afterwards "many ministers of the Presbyterian Church will proceed to decry that same Confession and that doctrine of the infallibility of Scripture to which they have just solemnly subscribed!"[50] Liberals were entering evangelical church bodies with whose doctrinal affirmations they did not agree while falsely claiming to do so.

2. Liberals were dishonest in appropriating Christian institutions and endowments.

Machen observed that the currently existing churches and other Christian institutions were formed by, and financially supported by, Bible-believing Christians. Later and current generations of Christians hold those properties and those funds in trust. For those later generations to utilize them in an effort that is directly contrary to the purpose for which they were founded is entirely lacking in integrity.

> The funds of the evangelical churches are held under a very definite trust; they are committed to the various bodies for the propagation of the gospel as set forth in the Bible and in the confessions of faith.

---

[48] Machen, *Christianity and Liberalism*, 111–12.

[49] Machen, *Christianity and Liberalism*, 162.

[50] Machen, *Christianity and Liberalism*, 163. The entire discussion runs from 162–72.

To devote them to any other purpose . . . would be a violation of trust.[51]

Southern Baptists have seen this dishonesty at work, in both ways, within the state of Missouri. First, in the use of "doublespeak" (the hiding of one's true convictions through the use of language in which the speaker intends one meaning while knowing that his audience will receive it with a different meaning). This has been common in Southern Baptist institutions of higher education, as shown in the well-publicized case of Ralph Elliott, Old Testament professor at Midwestern Theological Seminary in Kansas City in the early 1960s. Elliott was at the center of a controversy and lost his position because he violated the commonly-observed standard of "doublespeak" and wrote openly about his beliefs.[52] And second, within the Missouri Baptist Convention, there were attempts in the early 2000s by liberals to steal institutions and agencies (including Missouri Baptist University) which were established and supported by Bible-believing Baptists across the state. Only determined action by the orthodox churches in Missouri preserved most of those organizations for the Missouri Baptist Convention. Vigilance is required.

Social Transformation Is the Fruit of Gospel Proclamation by the Church

The "social gospel" was the name of a movement within liberalizing churches at the turn of the twentieth century and into its first two decades. It has been defined as "a movement dedicated to the reconstruction of society in accord with the ideal of the kingdom of God,"[53] with the kingdom understood as centered very much on this present age. The key to the movement, as defined here, is the goal of the "reconstruction of society" by humans, now undertaken as the primary mission of the churches. This represented a complete

---

[51] Machen, *Christianity and Liberalism*, 166. Leith commented on both aspects of this phenomenon in several places. See Leith, *Crisis in the Church*, xii, 31, 34, 52–53, 55–56, 113–14.

[52] For a brief summary, see Wills, *Southern Baptist Theological Seminary*, 406–10.

[53] Dillenberger and Welch, *Protestant Christianity*, 211.

reconceptualizing of the mission of the Christian church. Machen's response included the following emphases.

1. The primary mission of the church is gospel proclamation.

Elsewhere in his writings, Machen argued that apostolic Christianity was as follows: (1) it was founded on the OT revelation, which identifies the living and true God as maker of heaven and earth; (2) it proclaimed the universal sinfulness of mankind; and (3) it proclaimed Jesus' death and resurrection from the dead. He insisted that contemporary Christianity should do the same.[54]

2. The biblical gospel refuses to be used for any ends but its own.

The gospel of Jesus Christ has as its aim to bring humans into the knowledge of God, which is a sufficient end in itself. "Christianity," Machen said, "refuses to be regarded as a mere means to a higher end."[55] He continued, expounding the words of Christ in Luke 14:26, "If anyone comes to me and does not hate his father and mother . . . he cannot be my disciple":

> the relationship to Christ takes precedence of all other relationships, even the holiest of relationships like those that exist between husband and wife and parent and child. Those other relationships exist for the sake of Christianity and not Christianity for the sake of them. Christianity will indeed accomplish many useful things in this world, but if it is accepted in order to accomplish those useful things it is not Christianity.[56]

Machen wrote, "the worship of God has a value of its own. . . . According to Christian belief, man exists for the sake of God."[57] "If once a man comes to believe in a personal God, then the worship of him . . . will be regarded . . . as the chief end of man."[58] If knowing

---

[54] See Machen, "The Christian View of Missions," in *What Is Christianity?*, 148–55.

[55] Machen, *Christianity and Liberalism*, 151.

[56] Machen, *Christianity and Liberalism*, 152.

[57] Machen, *Christianity and Liberalism*, 154.

[58] Machen, *Christianity and Liberalism*, 153.

and worshipping God is man's chief end, then to substitute any other end as the goal of Christianity is to replace the greater goal with the lesser and to attempt to manipulate God, in this case, in the interest of transforming human society along the lines envisioned by mere fallen humans.

3. The ethical teaching of Jesus was not intended as a program for the transformation of human society at large.

Machen suggested that it is futile to apply Christian ethical standards to unregenerate people. Regarding Jesus' Sermon on the Mount, Machen asserted that "the ethic of the discourse, taken by itself, will not work at all."[59] A few lines later, Machen continued:

> The error consists in supposing that the Golden Rule, with the rest of the Sermon on the Mount, is addressed to the whole world. As a matter of fact, the whole discourse is expressly addressed to Jesus' disciples . . . persons in whom a great change has been wrought . . . which fits them for entrance into the Kingdom of God.[60]

We are not to expect a transformation of society wrought by the world's application of the ethic Jesus taught, for it is impossible for the world to obey it for "a blessed society cannot be formed out of men who are still under the curse of sin."[61]

4. The biblical gospel does in fact produce a transformed society; it is called the church.

The reception of the gospel leads to the formation of local communities of disciples committed to living out together their new life in Jesus Christ. Machen claimed:

> according to Christian belief, as well as according to liberalism, there is really to be a transformation of society. . . . [E]ven before the salvation of all society has been achieved, there is already a society of

---

[59] Machen, *Christianity and Liberalism*, 37.
[60] Machen, *Christianity and Liberalism*, 37–38.
[61] Machen, *Christianity and Liberalism*, 158.

those who have been saved. That society is the Church. The Church is the highest Christian answer to the social needs of man.[62]

The church, and only the church, will exhibit the new life of the kingdom of God during this age:

> It is upon this brotherhood of twice-born sinners, this brotherhood of the redeemed, that the Christian founds the hope of society. He finds no solid hope in the improvement of earthly conditions, or the molding of human institutions under the influence of the Golden Rule . . . Human institutions are really to be molded, not by Christian principles accepted by the unsaved, but by Christian men; the true transformation of society will come by the influence of those who have themselves been redeemed.[63]

As Machen has emphasized, the true mission of the church is centered in gospel proclamation, not social transformation. The NT holds out neither to Christians nor to churches the explicit aim of transforming the whole of human society; rather, it calls upon churches to portray among themselves the social transformation which the gospel brings about among redeemed humans. The transformation of society has historically occurred under the preaching and reception of the gospel, whether sooner or later. It will come soon enough, but it comes only as a product of the gospel's proclamation and reception.

It is possible to point to such transformed societies on a local basis. One such is Legacy Baptist Church of northwest Arkansas. There it is possible to observe ethnic diversity achieved without effort. Among a group of just a few dozen people, there are several Anglo families, a half-Hispanic family, an Asian Indian family, a black Nigerian, the Malayan Chinese wife of an Anglo husband, a half-Korean man and his Anglo wife, and all these with their children. And they love one another. It was the Anglo husband of the Chinese wife who marveled at the diversity—and unity—of this congregation without an overt attempt to achieve it. No "diversity officer" was necessary. It just happened because all are in Christ; as Paul said, "we are all one in

---

[62] Machen, *Christianity and Liberalism*, 159.
[63] Machen, *Christianity and Liberalism*, 158.

Christ Jesus" (Gal. 3:28). That is the social transformation which the NT envisions.

5. The biblical gospel promotes an alternative approach to social revolution for the alleviation of social maladjustments.

Machen identified what he saw as the apostolic and biblical approach to social issues. In *Christianity and Liberalism* to a limited extent, and in his *The New Testament: An Introduction to its Literature and History* to a much fuller extent, Machen outlined the approach taken in the NT to deal with social issues.[64]

Apostolic Christianity is not a social reform movement.
In Machen's thorough survey of the NT and its teaching, Chapter 49 is entitled "Christianity and Human Relationships." Here, in sections on "Society" and "Christianity and Social Service," Machen laid out in several subsections the method of approach to social problems observed within earliest Christianity.

In the first place, he observed that the early Christian movement did not focus directly on solving social problems at all.

> Social conditions in the apostolic age were exceedingly bad. . . . [H]owever, Christianity seemed to exhibit a remarkable patience in its attitude toward the evil institutions of the time. It made no loud demands for social equality; it indulged in no denunciations of slavery; it apparently assumed the continuance of the distinction between rich and poor.[65]

The point is that the Christian movement was not originally founded as an effort to address any social maladjustments or injustices whatsoever. It evidently had other aims.

---

[64] This outline is adapted from points made in J. Gresham Machen, *The New Testament: An Introduction to its Literature and History*, ed. W. John Cook (Edinburgh; Carlisle, PA: Banner of Truth Trust, 1976), 368–72. The headings are taken from this section.

[65] Machen, *The New Testament*, 368

The early Christians had no immediate power over existing institutions.

Machen said, "The explanation is to be found partly, no doubt, in the circumstances of the early Christians. . . . Those humble men and women were excused from instituting a social revolution simply because they did not have the power."[66]

The Apostolic Church had something better than social reform.

Machen asserted:

> The fundamental fact is that the Church refrained from a definite program of social reform simply because she had something far better; she postponed the improvement of earthly conditions in order to offer eternal life. . . . If a man has communion with the living God, all else can wait.[67]

Christianity is independent of earthly conditions.

The "spiritual and heavenly character of Christianity . . . makes the Christian offer universal. A gospel which promises merely an improvement of the world is dependent upon worldly conditions."[68] A person may be deprived of that improvement by "disease, or ill fortune, or unjust suspicion, or death . . ." Machen said, however:

> Christianity is a life in communion with God, and that can be maintained in poverty and in plenty, in slavery and in freedom, in life and in death. The Christian offer is extended to everyone, and every earthly condition, no matter how degrading or how painful, can be used in the service of God.[69]

Society or the individual?

Machen said:

> Evangelical Christianity makes its first appeal to the individual. . . . The first purpose of true Christian evangelism is to bring the individual man clearly and consciously into the presence of his God.

---

[66] Machen, *The New Testament*, 368.

[67] Machen, *The New Testament*, 369–69.

[68] Machen, *The New Testament*, 369.

[69] Machen, *The New Testament*, 369.

Without that, all else is of temporary value; the human race is composed of individual souls; the best of social edifices will crumble if all the materials are faulty.[70]

Every man should first correct his own faults.

Machen wrote, "There was nothing directly revolutionary about the apostolic teaching."[71] Rather:

> In the apostolic Church, every man was made to know his own faults, not the faults of other people. The rich were rebuked for their covetousness and selfishness; but the poor were commanded, with just as much vehemence, to labor for their own support. . . . [A]postolic Christianity sought to remove the evils of an unequal distribution of wealth, not by a violent uprising against the rich, but by changing the hearts of the rich men themselves. . . . [I[t cannot be said that the apostolic method is altogether antiquated.[72]

The ennobling of existing institutions

> A Christian man, [even a slave,] instead of seeking an immediate change in his social position, was first of all to learn to make the best of whatever position was his already . . . 1 Cor. 7:20-24. The freedom of the Christian, in other words, is entirely independent of freedom in this world; a slave can be just as free in the higher, spiritual sense as his earthly master. In this way the position of the slave was ennobled.[73]

The substitution of good institutions for bad

"In the long run . . . such conceptions were bound to exert a pervasive influence even upon earthly institutions."[74] Paul's instructions to Philemon concerning his runaway slave Onesimus would logically and naturally result in emancipation. "[S]uch was the actual process in the history of the Church. Slavery, moreover, is only an example; a host of other imperfect social institutions have similarly been

---

[70] Machen, *The New Testament*, 370.

[71] Machen, *The New Testament*, 370.

[72] Machen, *The New Testament*, 370–71.

[73] Machen, *The New Testament*, 371.

[74] Machen, *The New Testament*, 371.

modified or removed."[75] Machen cited Galatians 3:28 and affirmed that the "enunciation of great principles such as this . . . will finally transform the face of the world."[76]

6. Contemporary Application of Machen's Analysis of the New Testament Approach

Machen was right, and we Southern Baptists sorely need to take note of that fact. The biblical gospel did not originate as a social reform movement; it originated as a movement for human regeneration, justification, and renewal in fellowship with God under the preaching of the gospel and the operation of the Holy Spirit. At the most fundamental level what is needed is not social reform but renewed people, with changed hearts, who will then produce social change. We may properly seek to extend and apply Machen's principles to our current situation.

We ought to refuse to inculcate a spirit of victimization.
We should notice one great benefit of the NT approach to social issues as outlined by Machen: it gave people dignity, for it avoided the trap of promoting in oppressed persons an attitude of victimization. It is difficult to imagine the earliest Christians complaining about being victims of unjust policies or actions (see Acts 5:41; 16:25; although they did at times seek redress of legal injustices suffered, Acts 16:37; 25:11). The mentality of victimhood is unfortunately being encouraged by contemporary efforts of social reform, particularly the "social justice" movement; but a sense of victimhood produces a miserable, hopeless, and helpless perspective (which feeds off blaming others for one's misfortunes) or else a revolutionary mentality. This was not the method of apostolic Christianity. That which child psychologist John Rosemond has asserted about children is just as applicable to adults in our own society:

> The person who doesn't think before he acts [because he hasn't been allowed to bear the consequences of his own actions] can't figure out

---

[75] Machen, *The New Testament*, 372.
[76] Machen, *The New Testament*, 372.

why he does bad things and bad things happen to him. . . . [He] usually blames whatever it is on someone else. Blaming and complaining are his specialties. He's a victim, and by definition, victims are not happy people. By the way, victimhood is always a choice. The reason one is a victim is not found either in his body or out there in the world. Victimhood is in one's head.[77]

The biblical perspective does not foster a sense of helplessness and dependence in people by insisting on their victimhood at the hands of others, and thus demanding their deliverance at the expense of others. Rather, while acknowledging the reality of oppression, it affirms that we are all the victims of our own fallenness and depravity, a self-victimization which only the grace of God can remedy.

Primary emphasis on social reform distracts from the church's gospel mission.

Giving primary emphasis to social transformation distracts the church from its gospel mission. Machen had observed the liberal complaint that "The older evangelism . . . sought to rescue individuals, while the newer evangelism seeks to transform the whole organism of society: the older evangelism was individual; the newer evangelism is social."[78] He went on to address the complaint by pointing out that biblical Christianity does not ignore but "provides fully for the social needs of man."[79] But he insisted that "the Christian man believes that there can be no applied Christianity unless there be a 'Christianity to apply',"[80] citing here a contemporary defender of the historic gospel. The central issue was, in Machen's view, that theological liberalism left the churches with no Christianity to apply.

---

[77] John Rosemond, "Punishing children for bad behavior is not bad parenting," *Northwest Arkansas Democrat-Gazette*, January 14, 2020.

[78] Machen, *Christianiiy and Liberalism*, 152. In Leith, *Crisis in the Church*, 42, he draws attention to the social issues and causes which were distracting churches from the gospel during the 1990s. Such issues preoccupied the curriculum and teaching in the seminaries, as expressed in "the seminary's embrace of a multitude of causes," and resulting in what he calls a "loss of focus."

[79] Machen, *Christianity and Liberalism*, 153. For his treatment of the matter, see 153–55.

[80] Machen, *Christianity and Liberalism*, 155.

Machen did not live long enough to see the devastating effects of the social gospel on the liberal churches. But his instincts were correct. Those Protestant denominations which abandoned biblical authority and embraced the "social gospel" largely lost the biblical gospel. They abandoned the doctrinal content of Christianity; lost their Christian identity, commitment, and witness; capitulated to the standards of the prevailing culture; and have been experiencing sharp numerical and financial decline for the last several decades. These churches may soon disappear, having become irrelevant and superfluous in the contemporary setting as they parrot the current faddish causes. The social gospel as it flourished in the early twentieth century has been tried and found wanting; it failed as a basis for maintaining a vital Christianity.

The danger of alien ideological foundations is real.

Likewise, Machen could not have foreseen the situation we now face, a hundred years later. But he did recognize the danger of building the church's mission on alien ideological foundations. That mission was shifted from gospel proclamation to "the betterment of conditions upon this earth" based on the false ideology that "this world is really all in all."[81] The result has already been described. The current generation of evangelicals needs to learn from the history of the past century, for it appears that we are now facing a new "social gospel" in our own day, to which Machen's observations still apply. Perhaps the greatest immediate threat to the SBC and evangelicalism at large is its potential embrace of the current so-called "Social Justice" movement. If the SBC embraces this current movement, it could likewise lose its grip on the gospel and eventually become as irrelevant as the mainline denominations, for this movement, despite its name, is unbiblical and anti-Christian to its core. The most basic problems with this movement are: (1) It did not arise from the Bible but is only artificially attached to Christianity. Historian James Nichols has described the original "social gospel" as "a movement looking for a theology"[82]; the same could be said for the current "social justice"

---

[81] Machen, *Christianity and Liberalism*, citations from 149, 148.

[82] James H. Nichols, *History of Christianity, 1650–1950: Secularization of the West* (New York: Ronald Press, 1956), 280.

movement. (2) It does not represent the true biblical concept of justice (receiving what one deserves) but a foreign concept and becomes unjust in practice.[83] (3) It constitutes an alien ideology which is not consistent with the biblical worldview. The "Social Justice" movement, according to current historical analysis, is the offspring of "Critical Theory," an expression of Neo-Marxism (an ideology gaining influence in Germany during the 1920s at the University of Frankfort) combined with applied Postmodernism (initially a theoretical outlook emerging in the 1960s, but transformed into ideological activism from the late 1980s to about 2010).[84] Like Marxism and as an expression of it, "Social Justice" divides humanity into different classes of people, the oppressors and the oppressed (formerly, on the basis of economic factors; now on the basis of race, sex, and social class), pits them against each other, and it offers as the only remedy a radical transformation of the major social structures of civilization through revolution. The biblical reality is that all members of every social class and ethnic group are personally sinners in need of repentance, and that all members of any social class or ethnic group do not personally belong by definition to one or the other category of either oppressed or oppressors. As an analytical tool, Critical Theory offers a different analysis of the human condition than the Bible does.[85] (4) The movement represents the impossible attempt to achieve what Thomas Sowell has called "cosmic justice."[86] Such an effort requires an omniscience which is not available to finite humans; a power which is coercive and thus corrupting when placed in the hands of self-interested humans; and a perfect sense of justice which is lacking in fallen humans. The achievement of "cosmic justice" is possible for God alone, and it is certain that he will eventually accomplish it.

---

[83] See E. Calvin Beisner, *Social Justice vs. Biblical Justice: How Good intentions Undermine Justice and Gospel* (n.p., Good Trees Press, 2018).

[84] See Helen Pluckrose and James Lindsay, *Cynical Theories: How Activist Scholarship Made Everything about Race, Gender, and Identity – and Why This Harms Everybody* (Durham, NC: Pitchstone Publishing, 2020), 11–66, especially 47–48.

[85] For an introduction, see Melvin Tinker, *That Hideous Strength: How the West Was Lost, The Cancer of Cultural Marxism in the Church, the World and the Gospel of Change* (Welwyn, Garden City, U.K.: EP Books, 2018).

[86] Thomas Sowell, *The Quest for Cosmic Justice* (New York: The Free Press, 1999).

Conclusion

Machen's warning suggests that faithfulness to our stewardship requires (1) that we adhere to the historical and doctrinal nature of the gospel message; (2) that we be on guard against an anti-supernatural philosophy intruding itself into our churches and denominational institutions; (3) that we recognize that theological liberalism constitutes a different religion than historic Christianity; (4) that we be alert for liberalism's possible use of deceptive means to gain its ends; and (5) that we follow the NT pattern of evangelism and church life in our churches.

John Leith was so fearful of the perceived threat from the theological right ("fundamentalism") that he ignored the real threat from the theological left until it was too late.[87] If he and others who were concerned for Presbyterian orthodoxy had earlier paid more attention to Machen's strictures, perhaps the situation could have been saved. In that instance, we must say with sadness, historical developments have shown that Machen was right. If Southern Baptists desire to avoid the fate of the mainline Protestant bodies, we would do well to listen to Machen also. We do not want our history to tell the same story.

---

[87] Leith essentially acknowledged this. See Leith, *Crisis in the Church*, x.

THE DOCTRINE OF DIVINE SIMPLICITY
IN CONFESSIONAL LUTHERAN DOGMATICS

John C. Biegel[*]

In his examination of the state of divine simplicity in theological discourse, James Dolezal seeks to validate Richard Muller's claim that the classical theistic understanding of the doctrine has been among "the normative assumptions of theology"[1] throughout the history of the church. Dolezal offers "a brief sketch of what some of the church's leading theologians have said about the [doctrine of divine simplicity] in the last two millennia."[2] Through this survey of patristic, medieval, Reformation, and post-Reformation voices, Dolezal convincingly demonstrates that divine simplicity in its classical theistic form is the majority report across the ages and ecclesiastical branches of Christian theology—both Roman Catholic and Reformed Protestant.[3] There is one branch of Christianity, however, on which Dolezal does not comment, and that is Lutheranism.[4]

Confessional Lutheranism developed alongside Reformed theology in the sixteenth and seventeenth centuries, having broken from Rome over a myriad of theological issues principally related to Scripture, authority, justification, and the nature of the gospel. As vigorously as they distanced themselves from Roman Catholicism

[*] John C. Biegel, M.Div., The School of Divinity at Cairn University, is one of the pastors at Riverstone Church in Yardley, PA and a ThM student at the School of Divinity at Cairn University in Langhorne, PA, where he is writing his thesis on the reception and continuity of Marrow theology in the work of Scottish theologian John Colquhoun. The author wishes to express his gratitude to Dr. James E. Dolezal for his feedback on this article and his encouragement to pursue its publication.

[1] As quoted in James E. Dolezal, *God without Parts: Divine Simplicity and the Metaphysics of God's Absoluteness* (Eugene, OR: Pickwick Publications, 2011), 3.

[2] Dolezal, *God without Parts*, 3.

[3] Dolezal, *God without Parts*, 3–10; See also James E. Dolezal, *All That Is in God: Evangelical Theology and the Challenge of Classical Christian Theism* (Grand Rapids: Reformation Heritage Books, 2017), 50–58.

[4] This is, of course, not at all to say the Dolezal is unaware of Lutheran sources or positions, but merely to point out that he does not explicitly address the Lutheran witness in his work. Understandably, his focus is more on his own tradition.

and as vehemently as they denounced Rome's theological errors, Lutheran theologians, like their Reformed counterparts, generally did not see the doctrine of God as a primary battleground. This is because under the head of theology proper there was great continuity between the pre-Reformation theology of the Church and what was held by Lutheran theologians.

This study contends that confessional Lutheran dogmaticians followed the same basic trajectory as their Reformed cousins, and that confessional Lutheranism, like confessional Presbyterian and Reformed theology, has historically held to a classical theistic understanding of divine simplicity. If this is so, it adds further weight to the argument made by Dolezal and others that classical theism has been *the* historical position of the church, both prior to the Reformation as well as during and after the Reformation in all of western Christianity's major branches: Roman Catholic, Reformed, and Lutheran. This would further demonstrate that those who surrender the doctrine of divine simplicity do so without historical-theological support and in contradiction to classical orthodoxy.

To demonstrate this, we will first establish the basic contours of the doctrine of divine simplicity as formulated by pre-Reformation classical theism. This will provide a touchstone against which the Lutheran theologians subsequently examined will be struck to determine their consistency or inconsistency with the classical doctrine. With this as a foundation, we will move to discuss the position of confessional Lutheran dogmatics, beginning with the Lutheran confessions themselves. From there, we will examine the positions of three of the most important dogmaticians of the period of Lutheran orthodoxy (late sixteenth to early eighteenth centuries), and then two of the most important theologians in the confessional-recovery movement known as repristination theology (nineteenth century). In surveying the work of each of these theologians we will note key similarities, deviations, and developments in the classical doctrine as previously established.

The Doctrine of Divine Simplicity in Classical Theism

The doctrine of divine simplicity is, ironically, quite a complex theological locus, but for the purpose of this study it may be broadly summarized in four theses: 1) God is entirely free from all physical and metaphysical composition;[5] 2) God's essence is identical with his existence;[6] 3) God's attributes are identical with his essence, and thus with one another;[7] and 4) complex predications made of this simple God are made analogically.[8] We shall summarize each of these theses in turn.

The first and most basic thesis of divine simplicity is that God exists "without parts"— he is entirely free from both physical and metaphysical composition.[9] He is not made up of realities stitched together to make a whole. The doctrine of divine simplicity received its fullest and historically most important expression in Thomas Aquinas's *Summa Theologiae*.[10] All subsequent theologians are forced to deal with Thomas's thoroughgoing treatment of the locus. In Question 3, Thomas makes six denials of composition in God. According to Thomas, God is not composed of bodily parts, form and matter, supposit and nature, essence and existence, genus and difference, or substance and accident.[11] In case these categories do not cover every conceivable form of physical or metaphysical composition in God, Thomas then asks "Is there composition of any

---

[5] See Richard A. Muller, *Dictionary of Latin and Greek Theological Terms*, 2nd ed. (Grand Rapids: Baker Academic, 2017), 336, (hereafter *DLGTT*), "God is understood as being absolutely free of any and all composition, [which] includes not merely physical but also rational or logical composition."

[6] See Michael Horton, "God," in Daniel J. Treier and Walter Ewell, eds., *Evangelical Dictionary of Theology*, 3rd ed. (Grand Rapids: Baker Academic, 2017), 344, "For God, essence and existence are identical."

[7] See Muller, *DLGTT*, 336, ". . . God is not the sum of the divine attributes . . .; the attributes are understood to be identical with and inseparable from the *essentia Dei*."

[8] See Thomas Aquinas, *Summa Theologiae* I.13.5 in Brian J. Shanley, ed., *The Treatise on the Divine Nature: Summa Theologiae I, 1-13*, The Hackett Aquinas (Indianapolis: Hackett Publishing Company, 2006), 134, "It therefore must be said that names of this kind are said of God and creatures according to analogy, that is, according to proportion." All subsequent references to Aquinas's *Summa Theologiae* are from the Shanley edition. Bracketed numbers indicate Shanley's pages. References to *Treatise on the Divine Nature* are to Shanley's commentary.

[9] See Muller, *DLGTT*, 336; Dolezal, *All That Is in God*, 40.

[10] See Aquinas, *Summa Theologiae* I.3 [24–38].

[11] See Aquinas, *Summa Theologiae* I.3.1-6 [25–34]. See also Dolezal, *God without Parts*, 44–65.

kind in God or is God absolutely simple?"[12] To this he responds that anything that is composite "comes after its components and depends on them," "has a cause, since things that are distinct considered in themselves do not come together to constitute some one thing unless there is some cause uniting them," and "must be in potentiality and actuality,"[13] all of which are to be denied of God. If God were composite in any sense, he would be a caused, dependent being. He would not be the uncaused, independent, self-existing and unbounded fullness of Being that he is.

One of Thomas's principal denials is that God is not composed of essence and existence. Stated positively, God's essence *is* his existence. If God is not identical with his existence (as he is with his essence) then there is something standing behind God from which God actualizes his own existence.[14] But the classical assertion made by Thomas and others is that "what makes God *be* (*esse*) and what makes God be God (the divine essence) are the same thing."[15] This is to say that God "does not merely instantiate divinity as a particular concrete instance of it," as a human being would instantiate a concrete instance of humanity, but rather "He is divinity itself."[16] God is "not a *particular* being among others, not even the highest one: He *is* his being."[17] This cannot be the case for any creature, where essence and existence cannot be identical. The identification of essence and existence in God is a key affirmation that draws a sharp line between creatures and the Creator.

Another fundamental corollary of divine simplicity is that the divine attributes predicated of God in Scripture and theology are, according to God's mode of being, identical with the divine essence and, therefore, with one another. They are not elements that are somehow more basic than God and of which God is composed.[18] Rather, they are different ways in which we observe and describe the

---

[12] Aquinas, *Summa Theologiae* I.3.7 [35].

[13] Aquinas, *Summa Theologiae* I.3.7 [35–36].

[14] See Aquinas, *Summa Theologiae* I.3.4 [30–32].

[15] Shanley, *Treatise on the Divine Nature*, 209.

[16] Dolezal, *All That Is in God*, 41.

[17] Dolezal, *God without Parts*, 107; emphasis original.

[18] See Dolezal, *All That Is in God*, 42–43.

single, simple divine nature of God.[19] As Brian Davies has put it, "everything that God is *is God.*"[20] The identification of God's attributes with his essence (and thus with each other) is the result of the fact that "we need multiple terms to describe God since no perfection that we can think of is adequate to the divine essence."[21]

Alongside and closely related to the previous point, classical theism claims that the complex predications made about God in Scripture and theology, such as attributing to him a variety of perfections that appear to be distinct accidental properties within him, are in fact made *analogically*, rather than univocally or equivocally. To use univocal language in reference to God means to speak of God in such a way that "our worldly knowledge and speech apply to God in the same way as they apply to the realities of our world."[22] In such a case, the Creator/creature distinction is in danger of being collapsed as the incomprehensible God is made, in effect, a comprehensible, created being. To speak of God *equivocally*, on the other hand, is to make statements about God in such a way "that what we know and say about our world has no intrinsic relation to what we can know or say about God."[23] In such a system human beings cannot say anything truthful or meaningful about God at all.

Thomas's well-known Question 13 in the *Summa Theologiae* addresses these issues and poses the solution of *analogical* language. While God is incomprehensible, we can know and make true statements about him, because he himself has done so in revelation.[24] The realities to which they point are not unrelated (as in equivocism), nor are they identical (as in univocism), but rather refer to analogous realities that exist in God in a qualitatively different way than they do in creatures. This is because creatures use *creaturely* language in order to describe the Creator—indeed the Creator himself has revealed himself by means of creaturely language. And so, while we make

[19] See Shanley, *Treatise on the Divine Nature*, 203.

[20] Brian Davies, *Philosophy of Religion: A Guide and Anthology* (Oxford: Oxford University Press, 2000), 549.

[21] Shanley, *Treatise on the Divine Nature*, 207.

[22] Gregory P. Rocca, "Aquinas on God-Talk: Hovering Over the Abyss," *Theological Studies* 54 (1993): 642.

[23] Rocca, "Aquinas on God-Talk," 641.

[24] See Shanley, *Treatise on the Divine Nature*, 324.

statements about God using the necessarily complex and composite language of creatures, we must be careful not to assume that those statements map on to God's mode of existence in a one-for-one correspondence.[25] This discussion becomes especially important in its connection to the attributes of God—specifically, the manner in which we can make multiple predications about what God is like that seemingly make him into a complex being. The attributes are *not* merely synonyms for the divine nature or for each other (even though the attributes are identical with the divine nature), but rather according to our mode of conception, they point to distinct realities that are present in God absolutely simply and identically.[26] Analogical language is the means by which classical theists explain the multi-parted statements that we (and Scripture) make about God.

Divine Simplicity in Confessional Lutheran Dogmatics

With the basic contours of the classical theistic doctrine of divine simplicity in place, we may move to examine the consistency of confessional Lutheranism with classical theism. Lutheranism's theological identity is significantly shaped, as one would expect, by Martin Luther. For the present purpose, however, we are primarily concerned with the articulation of the doctrine of divine simplicity by, first, the Lutheran confessions, and second, and more principally, later Lutheran dogmaticians.

To demonstrate that the positions of *confessional* Lutheranism are basically consistent with classical theism, we must ask in the first place what the Lutheran confessions teach about divine simplicity. It is noteworthy that the Lutheran confessions do not contain much in the way of expanded statements on the doctrine of God, such as those that are more commonplace in Reformed confessions. The Book of Concord does set forth the Apostles' Creed, the Nicene Creed, and the Athanasian Creed as confessionally binding,[27] but it would seem that

---

[25] See Shanley, *Treatise on the Divine Nature*, 327.

[26] See Aquinas, *Summa Theologiae* I.3.4 [132].

[27] See F. Bente, ed., *Triglot Concordia: The Symbolical Books of the Ev. Lutheran Church*, trans. F. Bente and W. H. T. Dau (St. Louis: Concordia Publishing House, 1921), 31–35.

the Lutheran confessions were more concerned with highlighting areas where they were at odds with the Roman Church, and later, Reformed churches, rather than necessarily giving a full-orbed statement of faith. Yet such silence will prove a indicator that on the doctrine of God, however, the Lutherans remained decidedly catholic.

The first and most theologically comprehensive of the Lutheran confessional standards is the Augsburg Confession of 1530, penned primarily by Philip Melanchthon.[28] The Confession contains the most robust article in the Book of Concord on the doctrine of God. In it, Melanchthon writes that the Lutheran churches confess "that there is one divine essence, which is called and which is God: eternal, without body, without parts [Lat. *impartibilis*; Ger. *ohne Stücke*], of infinite power, wisdom, and goodness, the Maker and Preserver of all things, visible and invisible."[29] While some translations take *impartibilis* as "indivisible,"[30] Melanchthon's rendering of the phrase in German as *ohne Stücke* ["without parts/pieces"] helps the reader discern the theological assumption behind his statement.[31] It is more than merely to say that God cannot be divided (which could perhaps be read as a statement of the unbreakable unity of his parts), but that he cannot be

---

[28] See Timothy J. Wengert, "Melanchthon, Philip," in Timothy J. Wengert, ed., *Dictionary of Luther and the Lutheran Traditions* (Grand Rapids: Baker Academic, 2017), 492 (hereafter *DLLT*).

[29] Bente, *Triglot Concordia*, 42–43. The Latin statement in Philip Schaff, *The Creeds of Christendom, with History and Critical Notes* (3 vols.; New York: Harper & Brothers, 1878–82), 3:7 reads: "*Videlicet, quod sit una essentia divina, quæ et appellatur et est Deus, æternus, incorporeus, impartibilis, immensa potentia, sapientia, bonitate, creator et conservator omnium rerum, visibilium et invisibilium*" This statement is repeated almost verbatim in article 1 of the Thirty-Nine Articles of the Church of England. It appears in Schaff, *Creeds* 3:487 as follows: "There is but one true and living God, everlasting, without body, parts, or passions; of infinite power, wisdom, and goodness; the Maker and Preserver of all things, both visible and invisible." Schaff provides the Latin as follows: "*Unus est vivus et verus Deus æternus, incorporeus, impartibilis, impassibilis, immensæ potentiæ, sapientiæ ac bonitatis: creator et conservator omnium tum uisibilium tum inuisibilium.*" Furthermore, this language is closely paralleled by the Westminster Confession of Faith's "without body, parts, or passions." Schaff, *Creeds*, 3:606 provides the Latin as follows: "*sine corpore, sine partibilis, sine passibilis.*" This demonstrates some level of confessional consistency on theology proper between the Lutheran and Reformed churches.

[30] See, e.g., Schaff, *Creeds*, 3:7.

[31] See Francis Pieper, *Christian Dogmatics*, 4 vols. (St. Louis: Concordia Publishing House, 1950), 1:429.

divided because his existence is entirely non-composite—he has no parts into which he can possibly be divided.

The Augsburg Confession's statement on the doctrine of God was understood to be orthodox both by the Lutherans and their Roman Catholic opponents. The 1530 *Roman Confutation*, a Roman Catholic rebuttal to the Augsburg Confession, stated:

> When in the first article [the Lutherans] confess the unity of the divine essence in three persons according to the decree of the Council of Nicaea, their Confession must be accepted since it agrees *in all respects* with the rule of faith and the Roman Church.[32]

The Roman Catholic response to the Lutheran doctrine of God was thus one of agreement—the Lutheran position was the Catholic position. Melanchthon makes note of this in his 1530 Apology for the Augsburg Confession, which is also included among the Lutheran confessional standards and itself a response to the *Confutation*. He simply writes that "the first article of our confession our adversaries approve, in which we declare that we believe and teach that there is one divine essence, undivided, etc."[33]

Both the Lutherans and the Roman Catholics saw the Lutheran doctrine of God as being consistent with the classical theological formulation of the Church on divine simplicity. The one God, who is the Holy Trinity, exists "without parts." It makes sense, then, that Melanchthon and subsequent authors of Lutheran confessional documents did not find it necessary to elaborate or defend this position, nor did the Roman Catholic response challenge it. The confessional basis of Lutheranism, as understood both by Lutherans and Roman Catholics, assumes a classical theistic doctrine of divine simplicity. It would be left to later Lutheran dogmaticians to more clearly articulate the way the Lutheranism understood these matters. It is to these theologians that we now turn.

---

[32] *The Book of Concord: The Confessions of the Evangelical Lutheran Church*, ed. and trans. Theodore G. Tappert (Philadelphia: Fortress Press, 1959), 100, n.1.

[33] Bente, *Triglot Concordia*, 103.

Divine Simplicity in Lutheran Orthodoxy

Like Reformed theology, Lutheran theology entered a period marked by increasing dogmatic reflection using scholastic methodology during the late sixteenth and seventeenth centuries. This is known in Lutheran theology as the period of "Lutheran orthodoxy."[34] For the present study, we will consider three of the principle Lutheran theologians of this age: Johann Gerhard (1582–1637), Abraham Calov (1612–1686), and Johannes Andreas Quenstedt (1617–1688).[35] It was these three men who, in the evaluation of the modern Lutheran theologian Robert Preus, produced the two of the three greatest dogmatics texts "ever written by a Lutheran."[36] Along with others like David Hollaz, Gerhard, Calov, and Quenstedt have the distinction of being called by later Lutherans simply "the old dogmaticians."[37] How they articulated divine simplicity is of great importance for understanding the position of confessional Lutheran dogmatics.

---

[34] Robert D. Preus, *The Theology of Post-Reformation Lutheranism*, 2 vols. (St. Louis: Concordia Publishing House, 1970), 1:44. See also Kenneth G. Appold, "Lutheran Orthodoxy," in *DLLT*, 454–58. Appold notes that Lutheran orthodoxy was marked by "prominent commitments to the Lutheran confessions with biblical exegesis, an overt use of Aristotelian logic and metaphysics, and wide engagement with contemporaneous and historical authors" (454).

[35] One might wonder why one of Lutheranism's greatest theologians, Martin Chemnitz, is not included here. Preus has noted, that regarded as second only to Luther himself in his theological importance to Lutheranism, a statement that would argue for his inclusion (Preus, *Theology*, 1:48–49). Yet Preus, in *Theology*, 2:54 also states that when it comes to the doctrine of God, the early Lutheran theologians like Melanchthon, Selnecker, and Chemnitz did not "offer any discussion of the attributes of God, excepting in passing, as they expound their Trinitarian description of God." Despite Chemnitz's importance to Lutheran theology overall, the lack of extended reflection on the essence and attributes of God renders him less relevant to the present study.

[36] Preus, *Theology*, 1:62. Kenneth Appold in "Lutheran Orthodoxy" in *DLLT*, 455 likewise states that the works of Gerhard and Quenstedt, alongside Calov's *Systema*, were the most important dogmatics textbooks during the period of Lutheran orthodoxy. The continued use of these three works by the later repristination theologians demonstrates that they were still highly valued by confessional Lutherans beyond the age of Lutheran orthodoxy.

[37] See e.g. Pieper, *Christian Dogmatics*, 1:429.

1. Johann Gerhard (1582–1637)

Johann Gerhard was one of the most important dogmaticians in Lutheran history, "generally considered to be the third preeminent theologian after Luther and Chemnitz."[38] His massive work, the *Loci Theologici* (or *Theological Commonplaces*) is a masterpiece of Protestant scholastic theology. It is in Gerhard's work that Lutheran dogmatics finds its first serious engagement with and appropriation of medieval scholasticism to construct and articulate Christian doctrine.[39] Additionally, Gerhard was responsible for offering "the first extended and detailed discourse on the divine attributes in Lutheran dogmatics," on which previous Lutheran theologians had "left a real gap."[40] Gerhard's scholastic exposition of theology proper would become foundational for later confessional Lutheran dogmatics. In Gerhard, Lutheranism had its most thoroughly Thomistic dogmatician, both in form and content.

When Gerhard offers his definition of God, divine simplicity is the first truth mentioned. We quote the definition in full not simply because of its relevance to the present purpose, but also because of its remarkable breadth, balance, and beauty.

> God is an utterly simple spiritual essence, infinite, of limitless goodness, wisdom, and power; just, and truth—namely: the Father, who from eternity begot His Son, His image, who created and preserves all things through the Son in the Holy Spirit; the Son, who was begotten of the Father from eternity, who in the fullness of time assumed human nature and in it carried out the work of redemption; the Holy Spirit, who proceeds ineffably from the Father and the Son in eternity, who was poured out visibly upon the apostles and still today is sent invisibly into the hearts of believers, and who through the preaching of the Gospel gathers the Church from the whole human race and sanctifies it to the glory of God's name and the eternal salvation of those who believe.[41]

---

[38] Preus, *Theology*, 1:52. See also Benjamin T. G. Mayes, "Johann Gerhard" in *DLLT*, 283–84.

[39] See Preus, *Theology*, 1:53.

[40] Preus, *Theology*, 2:54.

[41] Johann Gerhard, *On the Nature of God and on the Trinity*, trans. Richard Dinda, vol 2 of *Theological Commonplaces*, ed. Benjamin T. G. Mayes (St. Louis: Concordia

But what exactly does Gerhard mean by saying that God is "an *utterly simple* spiritual essence"? As he explains this statement, his consistency with Thomas's account of divine simplicity, and thus with classical theism, is quite apparent.

> The essence of God is utterly simple, free of all composition, mixture and division, and, therefore, of all accidents. We prove this (1) From the removal of all types of composition. There are seven modes of composition: first, of quantitative parts as body. Second, of material and form, as an essential composite. Third, of genus and difference, as any species. Fourth, of subject and accident, as any created substance. Fifth, of actuality and potentiality. Sixth, of individual substance [*suppositum*] and nature. Seventh, of being [*esse*] and essence [*essentia*]. However, God is composite in none of these ways.[42]

Gerhard does not expand on these categories, which match Thomas's exactly, indicating that he assumes a Thomist framework for his doctrine of divine simplicity. He further affirms that God is "sheer and purest act"[43] and "pure actuality [*actus purus*]."[44] As a result "[God] has nothing of potentiality or passive potential mixed with Himself."[45] The thesis that God is pure act, without any admixture of passive potency, is a notably Thomistic distinction and a crucial lynchpin in classical theism.[46] Summarizing his position, Gerhard quotes from Rabbeinu HaKadosh in saying "Nothing is found in God that is not God Himself."[47]

Gerhard argues that God's simplicity acts as a doctrinal safeguard for God's perfection, absoluteness, and immutability. "[O]nly an

---

Publishing House, 2017), 98. The stereotypical accusation that scholastic theology is dry and dead melts away in the face of such an excerpt. One making such an accusation would do well to read another of Gerhard's statements from the subsequent paragraph: "There is not profit at all in subtle debating about God while meanwhile not loving the highest good, the substantial love [i.e. God himself]." These hardly seem the like words of an ivory tower theologian with a dry and dead faith.

[42] Gerhard, *On the Nature of God*, 133–34.

[43] Gerhard, *On the Nature of God*, 148.

[44] Gerhard, *On the Nature of God*, 93.

[45] Gerhard, *On the Nature of God*, 93, see also 148.

[46] See Dolezal, *God without Parts*, 34–41.

[47] Gerhard, *On the Nature of God*, 114.

incomplete being comes into compounding with another, because of its own nature it is suitable to compose with another incomplete being something more complete as both are compounded. But God is a complete and utterly perfect being."[48] If God were a compounded being, not simple, then in and of himself he would not be perfect, and there would be something outside of him, also incomplete in itself, that somehow made him more complete and perfect, and thus change him from what he was into something he will be. In short, there would be a measure of *becoming* in God. By further implication, there would also be another force acting to bring these parts together to complete God. But Gerhard affirms that God is "a complete and utterly perfectly being" and thus cannot be a compound being.

Gerhard is equally clear on the identification of God's essence and existence, a point which has significant implications for the Creator/creature distinction.

> All things created are composed if not of matter and form, then at least of actuality and potentiality, of being and essence. But only God's being [*esse*] is His essence . . . Whatever exists in God is not an accident of God but is His very being. Therefore He is the simplest being.[49]

This follows closely on Thomas's discussion of the same topic. Gerhard says much the same thing when he affirms that "in Him there is really no distinction between what He is and that by which He is, between Him who has and what He has."[50] He furthermore states that "God is . . . his own Being subsisting," echoing the Thomistic notion that God is *ipsum esse subsistiens* ("subsistent being himself").[51] His definition of simplicity, which among other things denies that God is a composition of essence and existence, is further strengthened by these unambiguous statements. In stating his

---

[48] Gerhard, *On the Nature of God*, 135.

[49] Gerhard, *On the Nature of God*, 8.

[50] Gerhard, *On the Nature of God*, 134.

[51] As quoted in Adolf Hoenecke, *Evangelical Lutheran Dogmatics*, trans. Richard A. Krause and James Langebartels, 3 vols. (Milwaukee: Northwestern Publishing House, 2009), 2:62. See also Dolezal, *God without Parts*, 93–94.

position thus, Gerhard explicitly identifies himself both linguistically and conceptually with classical theism.

The identification of God's attributes with God's essence is also affirmed in Gerhard's work under the locus of divine simplicity. Gerhard forms two theorems about the nature of the divine attributes in general. First, the attributes of God "in and of themselves [*in se ac per se*], are really and most simply one with the divine essence." [52] He goes on to say that this theorem depends on both 1) the simplicity of God, because his simple essence "excludes every composition of essence and accidents without exception," and 2) the immutability of God, because "if the attributes were in God like qualities, God would be made changeable because every quality and accident is present in changeable fashion."[53] He further states, "The essential properties in God . . . do not differ from deity itself but really [*realiter*, i.e. according to God's mode of being *in se*] are the divine essence itself. Therefore the essential properties of God prove no real difference in the deity."[54]

While it is affirmed that God's attributes simply *are* his essence, the second theorem Gerhard posits is that "for the sake of instruction and because of the weakness of our conceptual ability, the divine attributes are distinguished in various ways."[55] This is a key point and is picked up by later Lutheran theologians (though it is not original to Gerhard). The distinctions made in Scripture, or in our theologizing, about God's attributes do not describe God's mode of being *in se*, but rather describe the manner in which our finite minds can conceive of the infinite perfection of God's nature.

This leads into his discussion of analogical language. For Gerhard, "[I]t is one thing for something to be inherent in God accidentally, another for something to be said about God accidentally with an external predication."[56] Gerhard here affirms that our speech about God makes it sound as if God is composed of substance and accidents, but that this language does not correspond to God's mode of being. Rather, it is a matter of our "external predication," that is,

---

52 Gerhard, *On the Nature of God*, 114.
53 Gerhard, *On the Nature of God*, 114.
54 Gerhard, *On the Nature of God*, 93.
55 Gerhard, *On the Nature of God*, 115.
56 Gerhard, *On the Nature of God*, 136.

the statements we make about God's being according to how he reveals himself in his Word and works. After citing Conrad Vortius, who objected to the identification of God's attributes with God's essence on the grounds that Scripture asserts "that one thing and another are in God," Gerhard replies that "one infers clumsily that the essence and attributes of the divine essence really are different in God simply *because our mind conceives and considers them distinctly.*"[57] It is not that God is composed of parts, but that our conceptions and speech about the infinitely simple God are complex. As complex creatures, we cannot think and speak otherwise. Gerhard, both in form and content, was entirely consistent with the classical theistic account of divine simplicity, and his influence was evident in the next generation of Lutheran theologians.

2. Abraham Calov (1612–1686) and Johann Andreas Quenstedt (1617–1688)

The two most important dogmaticians in the generation after Gerhard were Abraham Calov and Johann Andreas Quenstedt.[58] Both men taught theology at the University of Wittenberg and both produced massive dogmatics texts. Calov wrote the 12-volume *Systema locorum theologicorum and* Quenstedt, who happened to be Gerhard's nephew, wrote *Theologia didactico-polemica sive systema theologiae.*[59] Although the bulk of both works await English translation, extensive references in Schmid, Preus, and others allow for an abridged account of their positions on divine simplicity. Like Gerhard, both men appear to have thoroughly imbibed a classical theist understanding of divine simplicity.

---

[57] Gerhard, *On the Nature of God*, 135; emphasis added.

[58] See Preus, *Theology*, 1:59, 62, where he calls Calov "the most brilliant and influential theologian of the silver age of Lutheran orthodoxy, a veritable pillar of orthodox Lutheranism" and says of Quenstedt's theological writing that "[o]ne might say Quenstedt's *Systema* killed systematic theology in the period of Lutheran orthodoxy as Michaelangelo killed Renaissance art by the unexcelled quality of his work. Quenstedt's lifework is so big, so complete, so concise and systematic, and so excellent that no latter Lutheran ever came close to equalling [*sic*] it."

[59] See Preus, *Theology*, 1:59–63; Robert Kolb, "Johann Andreas Quenstedt" in *DLLT*, 628; and Erin Lund, "Abraham Calov," in *DLLT*, 114–15.

On the topics of God's freedom from metaphysical composition and the identification of God's essence with his existence, Calov is most clear and concise. Following in the footsteps of Gerhard (and Thomas before him), Calov defines divine simplicity as that "according to which God is devoid of all real composition."[60] Furthermore, because God's being "is entirely free of all composition, therefore nothing accidental can happen to it."[61] Like Gerhard, Calov understands simplicity to include the denial of composition of substance and accident. He also holds to the identification of God's essence and God's existence. In a variation on a classical axiom, Calov states "*Nihil in Deo est, nisi esse, et Deus est ipsum esse suum*" ("There is nothing in God except being, and God is his own being").[62] The term translated here as "being" (*esse*) is the same term Thomas uses to describe God's existence, which is identical to his essence.[63] The statement implies that Calov holds to the identification of God's essence with his existence.

The proposition that God's attributes are God's essence is supported by both Calov and Quenstedt, and it is especially here that the latter is appropriated by subsequent generations of Lutheran theologians, along with the closely related topic of analogical language. Calov avers that "if [the divine attributes] really differed from the essence after the manner of accidents, a composition in God would be predicated."[64] Having already established that God is free from all composition and that "nothing accidental can happen" to the divine essence, one is not surprised to find Calov arguing that the attributes of God are not accidents, but are themselves the essence of God. "The attributes are by no means accidental, but on the part of the object, they are the essence of God itself."[65] The implications of failing to affirm the identity of God's attributes with his essence—to

---

[60] As quoted in Hoenecke, *Evangelical Lutheran Dogmatics*, 2:65.

[61] As quoted in Preus, *Theology*, 2:71.

[62] As quoted in Preus, *Theology*, 2:71, n. 41.

[63] See Shanley, *Treatise on the Divine Nature*, 208.

[64] As quoted in Heinrich Schmid, *The Doctrinal Theology of the Evangelical Lutheran Church*, trans. Charles A. Hay and Henry E. Jacobs, 3rd rev. ed. (Minneapolis: Augsburg Publishing House, 1899), 122.

[65] As quoted in Schmid, *Doctrinal Theology*, 121.

believe that God's attributes are accidental properties superadded to his essence—are serious indeed.

> For if [the divine attributes] were accidents, they would add a new entity or perfection and the essence of God would not of itself be complete. If they were to belong to God in the manner of accidents, God's essence would not be altogether immutable, because [it is] liable to accidents.[66]

Calov rightly echoes previous classical theists on this point. The simplicity of God guards truths like the immutability of God. If simplicity is abandoned, Calov states, immutability goes with it.

Quenstedt follows in the same vein when it comes to the divine attributes. He states:

> The divine attributes do not denote something added to the divine essence, but they are only inadequate thoughts about the infinitely perfect essence. The divine essence, like the ocean, is incomprehensible in all its infinite perfections, and the human mind cannot drain it out in one single thought, therefore with various thought we sip, as it were, something from that infinity.[67]

In this beautiful statement, Quenstedt not only affirms that the divine attribute and the divine essence are identical and divided only in our mode of conceiving God as he has revealed himself, but also demonstrates a developing tendency to foreground God's infinity as a basis for his simplicity. God's utterly infinite essence is simple, but because we cannot grasp such infinite perfection in a single concept, God reveals himself to us in various ways that all describe God truly, though not fully as he is in himself.

It is noteworthy that Quenstedt's discussion of the divine attributes is almost always tied to his thinking not only about the simplicity of God as a theological construct, but also how we think and speak about this simple God. In the above quotation, Quenstedt not only affirms that the attributes of God are not something accidental to, but simply are his essence, but also that the distinctions

---

[66] As quoted in Schmid, *Doctrinal Theology*, 121.
[67] As quoted in Hoenecke, *Evangelical Lutheran Dogmatics*, 2:72.

in the attributes are made solely in our conception, since we are unable to grasp God's perfect simplicity. He affirms this when he writes:

> Attributes are nothing else than inadequate conceptions of the divine essence, involving in part the essence itself of the object, and inwardly designating the same. Inasmuch as our finite intellect cannot adequately conceive of the infinite and most simple essence of God by a single adequate conception, therefore it apprehends the same by distinct and adequate conceptions, inadequately representing the divine essence which inadequate conceptions are called affections and attributes of God; affections, because they designate the divine essence; attributes, because *they are attributed to the same by our intellect.*[68]

But lest one think that this is mere nominalism, Quenstedt quickly argues that

> [a]lthough divine attributes are considered to be in God according to our mode of thinking, this mode of thinking is not without all foundation in reality. Nor are the attributes predicated of God only loosely and anthropopathically. But they truly and actually correspond to Him.[69]

Quenstedt means to distance himself from those who claimed that because the distinctions between the divine attributes are only subjectively present in our mode of conception and are not objectively present in God, they do not describe God truly. Instead, Scripture gives the theologian warrant to conceive of the attributes distinctly though these attributes are merely ways of describing the simple divine essence. Because those perfections that Scripture attributes to God are present in human beings only accidentally and imperfectly, we cannot conceive of them in any other way. Thus, while the language used of them is not univocal, it is also not equivocal.

When it comes to analogical language, Quenstedt is perhaps the most piercingly clear of the Lutheran orthodox dogmaticians, a fact

---

[68] As quoted in Schmid, *Doctrinal Theology*, 117; emphasis added.
[69] As quoted in Preus, *Theology*, 2:58.

that is not lost on later Lutherans. It is quite clear that Quenstedt has adopted the Thomistic distinctions between univocal, equivocal, and analogical language, and has opted for the third in his understanding of predications made about God.

> Essence, substance, spirit, and consequently the remaining attributes which are ascribed at the same time to God and to creatures, are predicated of God and rational creatures not . . . univocally, nor . . . equivocally, but . . . analogically, so that they belong to God [first] and absolutely, to creatures [second] and by way of dependence, analogy being properly thus employed with reference to an intrinsic attribute. The term *univocal* properly and strictly speaking, belongs to such things as have the name and the thing denoted by that name equally in common, no inequality interfering on account of the dependence on the one upon the other; *equivocal*, to such as have a common name but not the thing signified by the name; *analogical*, to such as have both the name and the thing designated by that name, but unequally, when the name and the thing belong to the one [first] and absolutely, but to the other [second] and by way of dependence.[70]

Though he does not mention Thomas, Quenstedt's concept of analogical language is thoroughly Thomistic.[71] Even more than Gerhard, Quenstedt is indebted to Thomas and classical theistic thought for his categories of language, which he employs for the same purpose as Thomas — to defend divine simplicity.

It is also evident that neither Calov nor Quenstedt believe divine simplicity to be merely a piece of doctrinal baggage left over from medieval scholasticism. Rather, the doctrine lies at the very heart of what Christians confess about God. Consider Calov's comment:

> If [the divine attributes] really differed from the essence after the manner of accidents, a composition in God would be predicated, and since, by nature, accidents come after essence, [the] former and latter in the order of nature would have a place in God, *both of which are contrary to the faith*.[72]

---

[70] As quoted in Schmid, *Doctrinal Theology*, 115–16; emphasis original.
[71] See Preus, *Theology*, 2:43.
[72] As quoted in Schmid, *Doctrinal Theology*, 122; emphasis added.

For Calov, to predicate some form of composition in God is not simply a theological error—it is "*contrary to the faith.*" The importance that Gerhard, Calov, and Quenstedt placed on the classical account of divine simplicity had a significant effect on later Lutheran theologians who sought to appropriate the confessional heritage of Lutheran orthodoxy, to whom we now turn.

Divine Simplicity in Repristination Theology

After the period of Lutheran orthodoxy, Lutheranism became increasingly influenced by Enlightenment rationalism on the one hand and Pietism on the other, and as a result, precise dogmatic theology largely fell out of favor among Lutherans.[73] But in the mid-nineteenth century there was a move among many Lutherans to restore the orthodox, confessional identity of Lutheranism that became known as "repristination theology." The repristination theologians sought to reinvigorate the Lutheran church by a strict return to the confessional identity and robust theological heritage of the age of Lutheran orthodoxy. They were marked by "fidelity to the Scriptures as the Word of God, the Lutheran confessions as the correct exposition of the Scriptures, and the theologians of Lutheran orthodoxy as unsurpassed standards of doctrinal precision."[74] In America, two of the most important repristination theologians were Adolf Hoenecke (1835–1908) of the Wisconsin Synod and Francis Pieper (1852–1931) of the Missouri Synod.[75]

---

[73] See Eric Carlsson, "Enlightenment," in *DLLT*, 221–22; Eric Carlsson., "Eighteenth Century," in *DLLT*, 210–23; and Appold, "Lutheran Orthodoxy," in *DLLT*, 458.

[74] John T. Pless, "Repristination Theology," in *DLLT*, 638.

[75] See David P. Scaer, "Francis Pieper (1852–1931) in Mark C. Mattes, ed., *Twentieth-Century Lutheran Theologians*, Refo500 Academic Studies 10 (Göttingen: Vandenhoek & Ruprecht, 2013), 20 and Pless, "Repristination Theology," 638. It is perhaps worth noting that the Wisconsin Evangelical Lutheran Synod and the Lutheran Church-Missouri Synod remain two of the most theologically conservative Lutheran denominations in America, whereas the Evangelical Lutheran Church in America (ELCA) is significantly more theologically liberal. One wonders if the efforts of repristination theologians like Hoenecke and Pieper (and others who followed in their footsteps like John Theodore Mueller) have had a restorative and preservative effect on the theological health those denominations.

1. Adolf Hoenecke (1835–1908)

Adolf Hoenecke was one of the leading theologians of the Wisconsin Evangelical Lutheran Synod in the later nineteenth century. While he did not attain to quite the stature of his contemporary and fellow German émigré Francis Pieper, he was "a very thorough theologian of a relatively old-fashioned cut."[76] He was one who was "thoroughly at home in Scripture, in Luther, and in Lutheran dogmatics."[77] As a result his theological works reflected the classical theism of his forebears.

In fact, when Hoenecke comes to define the simplicity of God in his *Evangelical Lutheran Dogmatics*, he essentially writes a commentary on the previous work of Gerhard, Calov, and Quenstedt, referencing each of them in turn: "The divine essence is most simple without any composition" (Gerhard), "God is devoid of all real composition" (Calov), and "God, according to his being, is most pure in actuality, permitting no contradictory force, no possibility of suffering; he is one to whom nothing can be given and who does not suffer anything from anyone" (Quenstedt).[78] Hoenecke does not offer his own formulation of divine simplicity, but rather allows his definition to rest in the old Lutheran dogmaticians.

Hoenecke cites Gerhard approvingly on the unity of God's essence. After stating that "God is not one only in number but also in essence," Hoenecke quotes Gerhard as saying: "God is moreover his own Being subsisting, unlimited by any modes: the same is notable to be divided either in actuality or in potentiality. Therefore God is in the highest degree especially one."[79] Here Hoenecke approves of the classical formulation that God is *ipsum esse subsistiens*—subsistent being himself. But lest this doctrine be thought to be merely a relic of scholasticism's Aristotelian categories, Hoenecke also opposes the claims of his contemporary, Lutheran theologian August Friedrich Christian Vilmar, that "the simplicity of God [is] a completely abstract

---

[76] August Pieper, "The Significance of Dr. Adolf Hoenecke for the Wisconsin Synod and American Lutheranism: Conclusion," *Wisconsin Lutheran Quarterly* 88:2 (1991): 143.

[77] Pieper, "Significance of Dr. Adolf Hoenecke," 143.

[78] Hoenecke, *Evangelical Lutheran Dogmatics*, 2:65.

[79] Hoenecke, *Evangelical Lutheran Dogmatics*, 2:62.

concept that did not come from Scripture but stems from scholasticism."[80] Hoenecke replies that, on the contrary, "our dogmaticians do consider the simplicity of God as a *scriptural* concept."[81] This introduces an emphasis that seems to be particularly important to the repristination theologians—the fundamentally biblical nature of divine simplicity.

The identification of God's essence and attributes receives a great deal of attention in Hoenecke's work. Here again his indebtedness to Gerhard is obvious. Indeed, the two theses Hoenecke proposes as necessary assumptions in his discussion about the divine attributes match Gerhard's two theorems. Hoenecke states in his first thesis that "God's attributes are in reality no different from God and his essence, but in truth and in reality they are one and the same with God's essence."[82] He clarifies that this means:

> God's attributes are not like the attributes of another being. With every other being, the attributes are first added to the being; thus, they are properly accidents that could be lacking without abolishing the being . . . In particular, humans can even have different characteristics and attributes that, whether they are present or not, do not change the continuance of the human being; thus the attributes are something objectively different from the being. This is not the case with God. His attributes are not accidents and cannot be accidents. If they were accidents, then they would, as particulars added to his being, add perfections to it, and thus his being would not in itself be perfect. But Scripture does not distinguish the attributes from the essence.[83]

If the attributes of God were somehow distinct from and added to his essence, then God would not be perfect, since something would be added to his essence and thus his essence would not be perfect in and of itself. He further states:

---

80 Hoenecke, *Evangelical Lutheran Dogmatics*, 2:65.

81 Hoenecke, *Evangelical Lutheran Dogmatics*, 2:65; emphasis added.

82 Hoenecke, *Evangelical Lutheran Dogmatics*, 2:71. See Gerhard, *On the Nature of God*, 114, where he says: "The divine attributes, as we consider them in and of themselves, are really and most simply one with the divine essence."

83 Hoenecke, *Evangelical Lutheran Dogmatics*, 2:71. Note again Hoenecke's emphasis that *Scripture* does not distinguish between God's essence and attributes.

> To speak accurately, God has not attributes that are distinct from his
> essence. He is simple, undivided essence, in which there can be no
> diversities of attributes or multiplicity of nature and manner,
> because that would immediately make God into a compound
> being.[84]

The implications of this are clear: if God were a compound being, he
would be no different than any other finite created being. Thus, the
identification of God's attributes with his essence is of primary
importance.

Hoenecke's second thesis on the relationship of the attributes and
essence of God also follows Gerhard's theorem exactly. Having stated
that the attributes of God simply are the essence of God, he says:

> [W]e human beings cannot grasp . . . the simple and infinite essence
> of God in all its fullness and perfection, and God himself cannot
> make us perceive or understand his essence in a way that is truly
> adequate to his essence. Thus, we grasp God's essence as he reveals
> it in Scripture—piecemeal, as it were . . . And these piecemeal views
> of God we call God's attributes.[85]

This statement leads into Hoenecke's discussion of the difference
between God as he is in himself and how human beings speak about
him. In this connection he reaffirms that

> the distinction of essence and attributes is not objective but only
> subjective in our thinking . . . Attributes are distinguished from
> essence not really, as if God consisted of essence and attributes, but
> only formally, insofar as the distinction is intrinsic *to our thinking and
> imagining about God.*[86]

It is not *in God* that the attributes of God are distinguished from one
another and from the divine essence, but rather according to our

---

[84] Hoenecke, *Evangelical Lutheran Dogmatics*, 2:71.

[85] Hoenecke, *Evangelical Lutheran Dogmatics*, 2:71–72. See Gerhard, *On the Nature of God*, 115, where he says: "For the sake of instruction and because of our conceptual ability, the divine attributes are distinguished in various ways."

[86] Hoenecke, *Evangelical Lutheran Dogmatics*, 2:72; emphasis added.

mode of knowing, conceiving, and speaking about God. This is quite consistent with the Thomistic notion of analogical language.

Yet Hoenecke is again at pains to show that while the distinctions we make between God's attributes in our God-talk do not have a one-to-one correspondence with God's mode of being, these distinctions are not meaningless because they are still made "on the basis of Scripture."[87] Because Scripture distinguishes between the divine attributes we are well justified in following Scripture in making such distinctions in our speech about him, though these distinctions are not *in God*, but only in our manner of predicating things of God analogically.

Like Thomas, Hoenecke also holds that merely because the attributes are identical to the essence *in God*, it does not mean that they are therefore merely synonyms.

> In no way is it true that the attributes are only empty names distinguished from the essence of God and from one another only by name, thus synonyms for one and the same thing, although in reality they are really distinct neither from God's essence or from one another. God's attributes are not purely subjective notions that have no real basis in God, but *God reveals himself to us in this way* so that we justly apply all the attributes to him. *But these attributes are not in God in the way we distinguish them from one another and apply them to God's essence.*[88]

This is very close to Thomas's statement that

> [the divine attributes] preexist in God as a unit and simply, whereas in creatures they are received as divided and multiplied . . . Thus although the names attributed to God signify one thing, nevertheless they signify it under many and diverse concepts, and so are not synonymous.[89]

It is according to our manner of knowing, not God's manner of being, that Scripture speaks of attributes in accidental language. This is not

---

[87] Hoenecke, *Evangelical Lutheran Dogmatics*, 2:72.

[88] Hoenecke, *Evangelical Lutheran Dogmatics*, 2:73; emphasis added.

[89] Thomas Aquinas, *Summa Theologiae* I.13.4 [132].

inaccurate or deceptive on the part of divine revelation, but rather a condescension to our conceptual abilities as finite creatures, and thus an act of grace.

Hoenecke, the Wisconsin Synod's leading theologian at the end of the nineteenth century, shows himself to have successfully appropriated the classical theism of Lutheran orthodoxy. He was not alone in the endeavor, however, and in terms of public notoriety and influence was surpassed by his counterpart in the Missouri Synod.

2. Francis Pieper (1852–1931)

Francis Pieper was the foremost theologian of the Lutheran Church-Missouri Synod at the end of the nineteenth and beginning of the twentieth centuries.[90] His *Christian Dogmatics* is a standard textbook for conservative Lutheran theology today. His deep concern for both biblical authority and a recovery of Lutheran confessional identity led him to the great "Scripture theologians" of Lutheran orthodoxy.[91] In both Scripture and "our old dogmaticians,"[92] Pieper found and embraced a classical theistic account of God's simplicity.

Like Hoenecke, Pieper is clear on the classical theistic thesis that God is entirely free from composition. "God's simplicity . . . is that attribute according to which God exists entirely uncompounded and without parts."[93] In this affirmation he follows Calov and Quenstedt, who root God's simplicity in his infinity.[94] Explaining the foundation for his understanding of divine simplicity, Pieper tersely states that "[t]he infinitude of God permits no parts."[95] For Pieper, composition implies finitude. If God were made of parts, he would be finite in some manner. This follows closely on the Thomistic understanding

---

[90] See Scaer "Francis Pieper," 17, where he suggests that Pieper was "arguably the most influential confessional Lutheran theologian in America" at the time of his death

[91] See his comments on Dorner as representative in Pieper, *Christian Dogmatics*, 1:439, where he says: "Dorner, as an empiricist and '*Ichtheologe*,' has discarded Scripture as the source and the norm of truth and therefore cannot follow the old dogmaticians, for they were Scripture theologians."

[92] Pieper, *Christian Dogmatics*, 1:429.

[93] Pieper, *Christian Dogmatics*, 1:439.

[94] See e.g., Hoenecke, *Evangelical Lutheran Dogmatics*, 2:63.

[95] Pieper, *Christian Dogmatics*, 1:439.

that the uncaused first cause must be simple and pure act, free from all composition. If God is infinite, he must be non-composite; he must be simple. Thus, unlike Hoenecke, who nods both to Gerhard's statements about God being *ipsum esse subsistiens* and to Calov and Quenstedt's statements about divine infinitude, Pieper appears to bypass the discussion of the identification of God's essence and existence, rather rooting the whole of his understanding of simplicity in the infinity of God.

The majority of Pieper's discussion about the nature and implications of divine simplicity is subsumed under his section on "The Relation of the Divine Essence to the Divine Attributes and of Other Attributes to One Another."[96] He states unequivocally:

> In God, essence and attributes are not separate, but the divine essence and the divine attributes are absolutely identical, because God is infinite and above space (1 Kings 8:27) and time (Ps 90:2, 4). Were we to assume that there are parts in God, we would ascribe finitude to the infinite God and thereby erase the difference between God and man. Therefore the Augsburg Confession says: God is 'without parts.' On the basis of Scripture the Lutheran dogmaticians have maintained that objectively, that is, in God, essence and attributes are absolutely identical.[97]

In this excerpt we see several of Pieper's key concerns tied together. He articulates his classical theism in stating that God's essence and attributes are "absolutely identical." He again clearly roots this statement primarily in the infinity of God, saying that the attributes and essence are identical "*because* God is infinite and above space and time." He touches on one of the key implications of divine simplicity—and on this point he is piercingly and perceptively clear—that if there are said to be parts in God, then God would not be infinite and therefore the Creator/creature distinction would collapse. And he draws together his three sources of authority: Scripture, the Augsburg Confession, and the Lutheran dogmaticians, who have "on

---

[96] Pieper, *Christian Dogmatics*, 1:428.
[97] Pieper, *Christian Dogmatics*, 1:428.

the basis of Scripture . . . maintained" these positions.[98] Such a statement plainly outlines Pieper's classical theistic account of divine simplicity, combined with his biblical and confessional Lutheran commitments.

Yet, just like Hoenecke and the older Lutheran dogmaticians, Pieper is quick to say that the identification of God's attributes and essence, while objectively true in God, does not mean that we are unwarranted or incorrect in distinguishing the attributes from one another in our theologizing. He is critical of those who "under the pretense that all the divine attributes constitute an indivisible unit" have ignored "the distinction between the attributes" and, as a result, "one attribute has been substituted for another."[99] In a notably Lutheran section, Pieper argues that, even though they are identical in God, the varied terms used to describe God's attributes of God cannot be synonymous on the basis of the distinction between law and gospel. For if God's grace *is* God's "remunerative righteousness" according to our mode of conception, then forgiveness of sins would be based on remunerative righteousness, rather than on the vicarious satisfaction of Christ applied by grace and received through faith.[100] This is a fascinating line of argumentation and one in which it seems Pieper is unique.

In addition to the law/gospel dialectic, Pieper argues for the non-synonymity of the divine attributes on the basis of analogical language in God's mode of self-revelation.

Since finite human language cannot comprehend the infinite and absolute simplex, God condescends to our weakness and in His Word divides Himself, as it were, into a number of attributes which

---

[98] Pieper's thoroughgoing commitment to the scriptural nature of divine simplicity can be further seen in a passage immediately preceding the above cited excerpt in Pieper, *Christian Dogmatics*, 1:430, where he says: "All theologians who claim to be Scriptural theologians will follow the dogmaticians [i.e., Gerhard, Calov, Quenstedt, et. al.]. For surely no Scripture theologian will seriously assume parts in God." This is a remarkable statement considering that opponents of divine simplicity, whether in the age of Lutheran orthodoxy (e.g., Socinus), in later theology (e.g., Dorner), and today (e.g., Craig and Moreland), all claim that divine simplicity is not a biblical doctrine.

[99] Pieper, *Christian Dogmatics*, 1:430.

[100] See Pieper, *Christian Dogmatics*, 1:430.

our faith can grasp and to which it can cling. . . . Because God employs our human language, He has also adopted our way of thinking and accommodated Himself to the laws of human thought processes, or logic.[101]

Like Thomas and the other classical theists, Pieper argues that statements made in human language, a creaturely artifact, are necessarily complex, in order to be able to reveal himself in such a way that human beings know, though not comprehend, his ineffable essence. This gracious condescension of God to reveal himself in human language and concept is done on the basis of analogy, rather than univocity or equivocity. Pieper addresses this issue as follows:

> In what manner can the same properties be ascribed both to God and to His creatures? Scripture supplies the answer: a) Not univocally, in the identical sense, as though the term and the matter apply to God and the creature in the same manner and degree (*univoce*); b) not equivocally, as though the terms when applied to God and to the creatures had no more in common than the sound, but in such case have an entirely different meaning (*aequivoce*); but c) analogically, similarly, because both being and attributes belong to God and the creatures, though not in the same manner or degree (*analogice*).[102]

Pieper's stance on analogical language is consistent with and indebted to Thomas's, and also quite clearly Quenstedt's.[103]

Analogical language is an essential component of our God-talk for Pieper because either of the alternatives lead to unacceptable conclusions. If we were to adopt univocal language, "then, strictly speaking, we would remove the essential difference between God and man. That would be tantamount to the deification of man." Yet if we were to claim that our language with reference to God is merely equivocal, "we would practically destroy all knowledge of God."[104] Here again Pieper shows his indebtedness to Thomas's conception of analogical language, for the Angelic Doctor says much the same thing

---

[101] Pieper, *Christian Dogmatics*, 1:428–29.
[102] Pieper, *Christian Dogmatics*, 1:431.
[103] See Schmid, *Doctrinal Theology*, 115–16.
[104] Pieper, *Christian Dogmatics*, 1:431.

in his discussion of the manner in which God is named by human beings.[105] Like Hoenecke, Pieper fully imbibed the classical theism of Lutheran orthodoxy, albeit with some of his own emphases and idiosyncrasies thrown in.

While these repristination theologians do not utilize the scholastic language and framework as rigorously as their predecessors, the content of their theology is the same. The work of both Hoenecke and Pieper reflect a classical theistic position on divine simplicity that is consistent with the theologians of the age of Lutheran orthodoxy, and in turn with the tenets of classical theism.

Evaluation

Having examined five of its key theologians, it can be concluded that confessional Lutheranism's dogmatic position on divine simplicity is thoroughly in line with the classical theism of both Thomas Aquinas and their Reformed cousins. There is significant consistency in confessional Lutheran dogmatics with classical theism on the core elements of God's non-composition and pure actuality, the identification of God's essence with his existence and God's attributes with his essence, and the use of analogical language to explain the complex predications made of this simple God in Scripture and theology. There are, however, some points of emphasis, variation, and development in the Lutheran account of divine simplicity.

The Lutheran dogmaticians especially emphasized divine simplicity at the point of the identification of God's attributes and God's essence. This is unsurprising, as this point is one of the fundamental corollaries of divine simplicity. Whereas others, like Bavinck, devote considerable space to discussions of God's absoluteness and pure actuality, the Lutheran dogmaticians refer to these theorems of divine simplicity, but devote much more space to conversations about the simplicity vis-à-vis the divine attributes. Especially for the repristination theologians, it is possible that the deep commitment to scriptural authority led them to devote more space to the relationship between God's attributes and essence

---

[105] See Aquinas, *Summa Theologiae* I.13.5 [133–35]. See also Rocca, "Aquinas on God-Talk," 641–42.

because this seemed more clearly biblical than the natural theological discussions about actuality and potentiality. One wonders if the repristination theologians' disillusionment with the prospects of human reason and reflection in the wake of the Enlightenment and its effects on Lutheranism led them to this emphasis. They certainly deeply respected and followed the fathers of Lutheran orthodoxy, but, as mentioned above, their use of natural theology and philosophical categories is significantly muted in comparison to their forebears (though it is not entirely absent).[106]

As just mentioned, exceedingly important for the Lutheran theologians, is the biblical basis of the doctrine of divine simplicity. Although they make clear use of natural theology and philosophical reflection,[107] they are also constantly at pains to demonstrate that this doctrine is thoroughly biblical. The repristination theologians were especially keen to emphasize the biblical basis for divine simplicity. While this was certainly not lacking in the earlier Lutheran orthodoxy, it takes on a more central role in repristination theology. Pieper's maxim is representative: "*Quod nonest biblicum, not est theologicum.* 'What is not Biblical is not theological.'"[108] In the same breath, however, he would affirm that the doctrinal conclusions of Lutheran scholasticism are thoroughly biblical.

This may also be why these later theologians appear to have been more comfortable taking divine infinity as a point of departure for the discussion of divine simplicity, rather than what might be thought of as more philosophical reflections on the nature of God's pure actuality.[109] Composition implies finitude, and finitude implies creatureliness.[110] Thus, for a being to be the infinite, uncreated Creator, it must be free from all composition—simple. For these Lutheran theologians, it seems they are more comfortable beginning a

---

[106] Pieper, *Christian Dogmatics*, 1:432, n. 62.

[107] Preus, *Theology*, 2:37 says: "Gerhard, like the other Lutheran dogmaticians [and here Calov is footnoted], envisages the pursuit of natural theology as the legitimate activity of the Christian as he applies the doctrine of creation."

[108] As quoted in Scaer, "Francis Pieper," 2

[109] See Gerhard, *On the Nature of God*, 98, 134; Quenstedt, as quoted Hoenecke, *Evangelical Lutheran Dogmatics*, 2:72; Schmid, *Doctrinal Theology*, 112; Hoenecke, *Evangelical Lutheran Dogmatics*, 2:55; and Pieper, *Christian Dogmatics*, 1:439.

[110] See Pieper, *Christian Dogmatics*, 1:441.

conversation from the point of God's infinity than by asking how God can be him from whom, through whom, and to whom are all things. This does not prevent Hoenecke and Pieper from following the Lutheran Orthodox dogmaticians in their theological conclusions, but their methodology is a bit different. God's infinity (the denial of finitude in God) is a negative way of expressing the positive statement of God's pure actuality (unbounded fullness of being), and for the repristination theologians may reflect a more explicitly biblical affirmation.

As with any theological tradition, there is variation and deviation from the mean. One certainly must remember that Lutheranism produced Isaak August Dorner, just as it did Johann Gerhard and Francis Pieper. Yet among those who were self-consciously in the stream of confessional Lutheran scholasticism, Muller's statement rings as true for Lutheran theology as it does for Reformed theology: "the underlying assumptions governing the doctrine of God during the eras of the Reformation and Protestant orthodoxy are very little different from those governing the discussion during the Middle Ages."[111] Inasmuch as Lutheranism is faithful to its confessional and dogmatic heritage (itself rooted in Scripture), it is thoroughly shaped by a classical theistic account of divine simplicity. This is further indication that deviation from classical theism in modern evangelicalism is to move away from the historic confession of the Christian church.

---

[111] As quoted in Dolezal, *All That Is in God*, 56.

Promise, Law, Faith:
Covenant-Historical Reasoning in Galatians
A Review Article
Brandon Adams[*]

Promise, Law, Faith[1] is the culmination of 30 years of reflection and teaching on Paul's letter to the Galatians. Author T. David Gordon boldly claims that "Paul's interpreters have not yet, in my judgment, correctly understood the Galatian letter" (13). He presents his interpretation as a *tertium quid* between the New Perspective on Paul (NPP) and what he calls the Dominant Protestant interpretation, noting that "mine could be regarded as a 'third perspective on Paul'" (24–25). The Dominant Protestant (DP) interpretation approaches the letter from a systematic-theological perspective focusing on the *ordo salutis* and concludes that "Paul's 'problem' with the law was exclusively or primarily due to an alleged meritorious abuse thereof" (1). Gordon repeatedly refers to this as reading *between* the lines in Paul's letter rather than reading the lines themselves. While he affirms the DP understanding of the *ordo salutis* and justification by faith alone, Gordon commends the NPP for challenging the DP interpretation of Galatians, arguing from a more sociological perspective that "Paul's difficulty with the law is motivated largely, primarily, or even exclusively by the reality that the law segregated Jews from Gentiles" (2).

Both interpretations, however, fail to adjust their thinking to Paul's thoroughly covenant-historical thinking. Twentieth-century Pauline studies "profited greatly by complementing such [systematic] studies with biblical-theological or redemptive-historical considerations of a *historia salutis* nature" (3). Gordon sees himself carrying this approach a step further, focusing specifically on *historia testamentorum* — the history of God's various covenanting acts. Such an

---

[*] Brandon Adams is a member of Northwest Gospel Church, Vancouver, WA.
[1] T. David Gordon, *Promise, Law, Faith: Covenant-Historical Reasoning in Galatians* (Peabody, MA: Hendrickson Academic, 2019).

approach recognizes Paul's use of three synecodoches to refer to three different covenants.

> [F]or Paul in Galatians, "law" is ordinarily a synecdoche for the Sinai covenant-administration, an administration characterized by law-giving. And "promise" in the same letter is ordinarily a synecdoche for the Abrahamic covenant-administration, a covenant characterized by promise-giving . . . Paul often uses a third synecdoche, "faith," to refer to the new covenant. He does so because it is a covenant characterized by faith in the dying-and-rising Christ . . . So, then, ordinarily when Paul speaks in Galatians of promise, law, and faith, he means the Abrahamic covenant (characterized by promise-giving), the Sinai covenant (characterized by law-giving), and the new covenant (characterized by faith in the dying-and-rising Christ); but we (mistakenly) hear him speaking of general theological categories/realities of God's pledges, God's moral demands, and our faith in such a God. (11)

Both NPP and DP's failure to recognize this leads to "monocovenantalism," referring instead to "the covenant" (NPP) or "the covenant of grace" (DP) in the singular, and thus misreading Galatians as a whole.

Introductory and Historical Matters

Gordon clarifies that his volume is not a commentary on Galatians but an endeavor to explain the argument or thought of the letter (the forest, rather than the trees). The first chapter introduces key issues including ὁ νόμος ("the law" or "law") as a synecdoche for the Sinai covenant, covenant-historical argumentation, and the idea that "Paul does not argue *for* the doctrine of justification by faith in the letter; rather, he argues *from* the doctrine of justification by faith" (42). Gordon argues that debate over justification during the reformation period led Luther, Calvin, and others to mistakenly assume Paul's debate was the same as theirs. Justification by faith alone was not in dispute at Galatia, so Paul reasoned *from* it to resolve what was disputed: whether Gentiles must be circumcised. That is, the problem in Galatia was the *practice* of the Judaizers, not the *doctrine* or *theory* behind the practice.

Chapter 2 addresses historical questions pertinent to Galatians and biblical interpretation, to which Gordon is "self-consciously somewhat agnostic" (50). "What we ordinarily call 'historical knowledge,' therefore, is substantially speculative or theoretical" (48). Since the biblical text is "what we actually have before us" (48), it "should have veto power over all the theoretical constructs surrounding it" (48). Gordon appeals to the concept of the *analogy of Scripture* (without naming it).[2] If the meaning of any given passage in Scripture is ambiguous "that ambiguity can be resolved better by reference to what is less disputable [another passage] . . . than to what is merely suppositional and therefore more disputable [historical studies]" (50). While this would appear to be a criticism aimed at NPP, Gordon actually directs it against DP. He singles out Calvin for "reading between the lines some historical thing the lines themselves do not say" (50), specifically Calvin's opinion that Paul "does not confine himself entirely to Ceremonies, but argues generally about Works, otherwise the whole discussion would be trifling."[3] Throughout the volume, Gordon refers back to this statement from Calvin as the epitome of the DP error, which assumed "that Palestinian Judaism taught a meritorious theory of justification" (17–18). In reality, Gordon's criticism on this point is against Calvin's application of the *analogy of faith*.[4] It would seem Calvin's understanding of the old covenant and its ceremonies informed his

---

[2] Richard A. Muller, *Dictionary of Latin and Greek Theological Terms: Drawn Principally from Protestant Scholastic Theology*, Second Edition (Grand Rapids: Baker Academic, 1985, 2017), 25, defines the analogy of Scripture as follows: "[T]he interpretation of unclear, difficult, or ambiguous passages of Scripture with a collation, or gathering, of clear and unambiguous passages or 'places' (*loci*) that refer to the same teaching or event."

[3] John Calvin, *Commentaries on the Epistles of Paul to the Galatians and Ephesians* (Grand Rapids: Baker Book House, 1979), 18.

[4] Muller, *Dictionary of Latin and Greek Theological Terms*, 25, defines the analogy of faith as follows: "[T]he use of a general sense of the meaning of Scripture, resting in Romans 12:6 and constructed from the clear or unambiguous *loci* (q.v. *locus*), as the basis for interpreting unclear or ambiguous texts. As distinct from the more basic *analogia Scripturae* (q.v.), the *analogia fidei* presupposes a sense of the theological meaning of Scripture. Sometimes the *analogia fidei* is understood to use a *regula fidei*, viz., a creedal form, typically the Apostles' Creed, as a basis for interpretation."

quoted statement, rather than extra-biblical historical studies of Second Temple Judaism.

On the DP reading, "Paul's positive statements contain his true thinking about the law itself, as delivered at Sinai, and his negative statements about it express his thinking about a later meritorious/legalistic abuse of it in the first century" (52). Gordon agrees with E. P. Sanders that this was a caricature of Second Temple Judaism, which did emphasize the condition of obedience in some places but elsewhere emphasized God's grace and mercy. He argues that his covenant-historical interpretation explains "why both E. P. Sanders and his opponents appear to be able, at times, to muster textual evidence for their point of view" (54): Second Temple Judaism was attempting to make sense of living under multiple different covenants, notably the Abrahamic (promissory) and Sinaitic (law). NPP, however, wrongly sees these covenants as one and is therefore unable to make sense of Second Temple Judaism.

The Argument of Paul's Letter to the Galatians

1. Galatians 1–2

Chapter 3 begins Gordon's discussion of the text itself, covering Galatians 1–2. "Both the Pauline gospel and his apostolic authority to proclaim it came from Christ himself and not from any mere human agent or agents" (63) (such as other Jews or even Apostles). Paul is not trying to please men (unlike Peter). Judaism (Paul's former life) refers not simply to "general faith in the God of Abraham and Moses, but zealous insistence on the Gentile-excluding dimensions of the Mosaic law" (68). Though Gordon does not believe the Galatian error is a doctrinal one, he does recognize that "nothing less than the gospel itself is at stake" (64) because if Gentiles have to become Jews, then the third Abrahamic promise to bless all nations in Abraham (the gospel) remains unfulfilled. The DP error was to understand "the gospel" too narrowly as referring to justification by faith alone (which was not at stake).

Many falsely assume that Judaizers were a well-known Jewish phenomenon or party and that they taught a false doctrine of justification. In reality, ἰουδαΐζειν ("live like Jews"; Gal. 2:14, ESV) was not a well-established term and may even have been coined by Paul himself. Gordon argues "that Paul does not say anything here about *'believing* like a Jew' but about *'living* like a Jew'" (57), indicating that the problem was practical, not doctrinal. The word is used only once in the NT (Gal. 2:14) and only once in the LXX (Esth. 8:17) where a literal translation would read *"were circumcized* and lived as Jews" (58). The same is found in an intertestamental example from Theodotus.

> In none of the examples is anything explicitly said about salvation, justification, or any other doctrinal matter at all. It appears to mean something like this: "Identify oneself as a Jew by performing the requisite marking ceremonies, to appease those Jews who would be scandalized otherwise." (59)

Paul's encounter with Peter was a separate, subsequent event from the Jerusalem Council. One reason for distinguishing the two events is that the Jerusalem Council was about "correcting doctrine" (Acts 15:1), whereas Paul's encounter with Peter was about "correcting behavior." "Peter's behavior of withdrawing from them [Gentiles] — as though they were still unclean and/or 'strangers to the covenants of promise' (Eph. 2:12) — denied that Christ, Abraham's single 'seed' (Gal. 3:16), had brought them blessedness" (88).

An important aspect of Gordon's interpretation is properly distinguishing the "we" and the "you" throughout the letter. Galatians 2:15 ("We who are Jews by birth [φύσει Ἰουδαῖοι] and not Gentile sinners.") clearly identifies the "we" as Jews (whether Christian or not), and 3:1 identifies "you" as Gentile Galatians. "What this [Jewish] heritage knew, according to Paul, was this: 'that a person is not justified by works of the law'" (92). This was known to the Jews by the existence of the atonement system and by their history (exile). Gordon notes that this is "simply incompatible with the dominant Protestant approach, which for many generations claimed that first-century Palestinian Judaism (Ἡμεῖς φύσει Ἰουδαῖοι) commonly taught that people were justified by observing the Mosaic law" (94-95). He suggests this drove translations such as ESV/NRSV to "avoid/evade the matter" (92) by suggesting these Jews knew they were not justified by works of the law *in spite of* their Jewish heritage ("yet we know"). Such a translation errs not simply on textual grounds, but rhetorical grounds as well. "If Paul were to assert as a commonplace (among those who were Jews by heritage) a belief that in fact was commonly disputed, his argument would lose all its force" (94).

Paul's statements on the doctrine of justification by faith alone in 2:15-17 "were largely reminders of what was already known. The Galatians would not have disputed Paul's fourfold denial that justification came through observing the law" (96).

Verses 18-21 are not autobiographical of Paul's personal *experience*, but rhetorical. "If I rebuild what I tore down, I prove myself to be a transgressor" (Gal. 2:18) refers not to Paul but to Peter re-establishing the dividing wall between Jew and Gentile by withdrawing from the Gentiles. "If Peter now regards the Kashrut laws as obligatory, then all of his previous violations of those laws count as transgressions" (103). "For through the law I died to the law, so that I might live to God" (Gal. 2:19) refers to the fact that the Torah (book of the covenant) testifies that the Sinai covenant was temporary, "even parenthetical" (101) as Paul demonstrates in chapter 3.

> Paul's reasoning is *covenant*-historical, not *personal*-historical . . . [I]t was not Paul's frustrated efforts at self-justification (Luther?) that caused him to die to the law… It was the law's own teaching about its temporary character that caused him to expect a day to arrive when its tutelage would end. If Torah teaches that God pledged to Abraham to bless all the nations/Gentiles through one of his descendants, then a later covenant (430 years later) that excludes Gentiles *must* be temporary. (102)

Life in Christ means death to Mosaic law. Christ and Mosaic law present two antithetical options. "If justification were through the law, then Christ died for no purpose" (Gal. 2:21) and we must therefore set aside the grace of God. "Paul's reasoning here (as elsewhere in Galatians) is all or nothing: Either we observe ὁ νόμος in its entirety or not at all. We either live to Torah in its entirety or we die to Torah in its entirety" (103).

2. Galatians 3:1–5

Paul shifts from the first-person plural ("we") and the first-person singular ("I") to the second-person plural ("you") "distinguishing himself from the (predominately Gentile) Galatians and their behavior. The 'you/we' throughout Galatians 3 continues to distinguish the predominately Gentile Galatians from Jewish Christians, as at Ephesians 2" (105). Paul asks the Galatians why they would turn to the Sinai covenant. The Spirit they received was an eschatological gift, but the Sinai covenant "was associated, temporally, with sin and the flesh, with the pre-eschatological order" (107). They received this Spirit through faith, not through the Sinai covenant. "Paul effectively reminded the Galatians that they had already experienced the realities of the age to come. Why would they now live as though that moment had not dawned?" (107).

3. Galatians 3:6–9

In verse 6, Abraham is introduced for the first time. "Paul begins his temporalizing/relativizing argument regarding the Sinai covenant, by establishing some of the realities of the covenant that antedated it" (109). First, he equates ("Just as") the Galatians' reception of the Spirit through hearing with faith with Abraham's justification through hearing with faith. Therefore, with regards to the inheritance of justification, "Those who have faith (whether Jew or Gentile) are Abraham's children" (110). And this very truth was preached to Abraham long ago when God told him, "In you shall all the nations be blessed." "[T]he particular 'blessing' pledged to the nations through Abraham was the justification that would come through the Christian 'gospel'" (110).

4. Galatians 3:10–14

Moving on to verse 10 ("For all who rely on works of the law are under a curse"), Gordon laments as follows:

> Most contemporary English translations obscure the parallel with the previous verse. The KJV was closer to preserving the parallel:

"They which be of faith [οἱ ἐκ πίστεως] are blessed with faithful Abraham. For as many as are of the works of the law ["Οσοι γὰρ ἐξ ἔργων νόμου] are under the curse." Those who are "of faith" are blessed with faithful Abraham; those who are "of the works of the law" live under threats of curse. (116)

These translations create significant problems for properly understanding Paul. Gordon says:

> The translation suggests that some attitude or idea about the works of the law brings a curse, when Paul's point is that the covenant administration in Deuteronomy 27 itself threatens twelve curses . . . It is not one's posture, attitude, or idea about the law that places anyone "under a curse": it is the Sinai covenant administration itself, as mediated to the Israelites through the hand of Moses and the Levites, that places Israel under a threat of curse. (118)

This is directly related to the DP interpretation, which argues that the curse stems from a misunderstanding of the law resulting in a legalistic pursuit thereof. But this is contrary to Paul's purpose in this passage, which Gordon argues is to demonstrate five differences between the Abrahamic covenant and the Sinai covenant — those who are characterized by faith compared to those who are characterized by works of the law; one includes the nations while the other excludes them; one blesses while the other curses; one justifies while the other does not; one is based on promise, the other on law.

Paul then quotes Leviticus 18:5 to prove that the Sinai covenant was not characterized by faith ("not of faith"). Rather, it promised blessing in the land of Canaan for obedience and threatened curse in the land for disobedience. This is in contrast to the Abrahamic covenant, which required only that Abraham believe.

Commenting on verse 13, Gordon maintains his view that "us" refers to Jewish Christians. He argues "the 'curse' referred to here is the curse previously spoken of: the threatened [temporal] curse sanction of the Sinai covenant, to which the twelve tribes of Israelites attached their ceremonial 'Amen,' and to which no Gentiles attached theirs" (125). Thus, the verse does not refer to the Gentiles' redemption in Christ, nor to the Jews' eternal redemption in Christ. Rather, it refers to the termination of the Sinai covenant by Christ's death delivering Jewish Christians from being under its threatened temporal curse. "While I affirm the theological truth of penal substitution, I do not believe Paul appeals to it here" (129). Gordon's explanation of how Christ being cursed (per Deut. 21:22–23) leads to the termination of the Sinai covenant is not lucid to me. If I have understood him correctly, he believes the curse-factor is actually irrelevant because "There was no provision in the Sinai administration for a representative human substitute to shed blood for others" (129). What did matter was that Christ's death actually inaugurated the new covenant because "there was provision in the Sinai administration for the shedding of blood to inaugurate a covenant" (129). This led to the termination of the Sinai covenant because of the fact "that one covenant is terminated when another is inaugurated" (129). Christ did not redeem Jewish Christians from the curse of the Sinai covenant by bearing that curse in their place. Rather, he redeemed Jewish Christians from the threatened curse of the Sinai covenant by dying (by means of a cursed execution) in order to inaugurate the non-threatening new covenant that would then terminate the Sinai covenant, delivering them from its threatened curse.

In verse 14, "Paul mentions two things that will attend the eschaton: Gentiles will receive the blessings [sic] pledged to Abraham, and the Jews will receive the promised Spirit" (130). Paul refers only to a single Abrahamic blessing even though the Abrahamic covenant included multiple. Gordon says, "Because Paul is referring here and throughout Galatians to the third pledge God made to Abraham: that through Abraham's seed, all nations/families of the earth would be 'blessed'" (130). The other two promises (to become numerous and to inherit a land) were previously fulfilled in Israel.

5. Galatians 3:15–18

In verse 15, Paul employs an *a fortiori* argument from human to divine covenants. If even human covenants cannot be annulled by subsequent covenants, then the Sinai covenant cannot annul the Abrahamic covenant. Paul then demonstrates (v. 16) that "The (third aspect of the) promise to Abraham will be fulfilled by one individual descendant of Abraham" (134). Paul's argument rests upon whether the referenced seed in the Abrahamic promises was plural or singular. Both the Hebrew (לְזַרְעֲךָ) and the LXX Greek (σπέρμα) are inconclusive, allowing either a plural or a singular meaning. Gordon explains that

> Paul surely understood that the first pledge to Abraham's "seed" was manifestly corporate and numerous; Yahweh would make his "seed" as numerous as the sands of the sea or the stars of the sky. Paul probably understood the second pledge to be corporate and numerous also: that to this large group of descendants a great, arable land would be given (after all, a single descendant could hardly inhabit/cultivate or militarily defend such a large piece of real estate). But he understood the third pledge singularly, as finding its focus in one particular descendant of Abraham. (135)

Gordon argues that Paul likely interpreted the third promise in light of Genesis 3:15 and 4:25, in which "seed" has a singular understanding. However, he also argues (contrarily, it seems) that Paul suggested "not so much a 'singular' reading of τῷ σπέρματι, but a focal reading, a concentrated reading" (136), following Calvin's argument that the meaning of Abraham's "seed" progressively narrowed over time until it came to refer only to Christ. Surprisingly, Gordon does not reference C. John Collins' study of Genesis 3:15,[5] T. Desmond Alexander's subsequent study of Genesis 22:18,[6] nor Collins' concluding follow-up on Galatians 3:16,[7] which collectively demonstrate that the original grammar of Genesis 22:18 indicates a singular referent and that this is what Paul was referring to (which supports Gordon's interpretation better than the "focal" reading, which does not depend upon a distinction between the three Abrahamic promises).

We then arrive at a foundational section of the volume, what Gordon calls the whole letter in a nutshell. He notes that "Both

---

[5] Jack Collins, "A Syntactical Note (Genesis 3:15): Is the Woman's Seed Singular or Plural?" *Tyndale* Bulletin 48:1 (1997): 139–48.

[6] T. Desmond Alexander, "Further Observations on the Term 'Seed' in Genesis," *Tyndale Bulletin* 48:2 (1997): 363–67.

[7] C. John Collins, "Galatians 3:16: What Kind of Exegete was Paul?" *Tyndale Bulletin* 54:1 (2003): 75–86.

lexically and rhetorically, my reading of Galatians is profoundly influenced by" 3:17–18 (137).

> Lexically, it is difficult to construe ὁ νόμος here as anything but the Sinai *covenant* itself, a covenant that was made at least 430 years after the previous covenant made with Abraham. My interpretation of the letter, then, suggests that this definition is the controlling definition elsewhere in the letter, unless some contextual consideration suggests otherwise. (137)

A key argument from Gordon is that no other suggested meaning of ὁ νόμος makes sense in this passage (and that meaning carries throughout the rest of the letter). In verse 17, ὁ νόμος cannot mean legalism (DP), God's moral will (DP, WCF 19:1-2), nor identity markers (NPP). "What came 430 years after a 'previously ratified *covenant*' was another *covenant*" (138) that was different in kind from the promissory Abrahamic covenant. "The law, whose recipients live under the threatened curse sanction, cannot be the means of inheriting the blessings that were promised to Abraham without corrupting entirely what 'promise' means." (140).

6. Galatians 3:19–22

Why then the *covenant* (v. 19)? "He is not asking (as we so often do) the general *theological* question of what all the law accomplishes" (142), therefore the answer is not "to reveal transgressions" nor "to restrain transgressions." Rather, it was to preserve the Abrahamic lineage until the promised offspring would come by separating them from the Gentiles and threatening curses against intermarriage with the *am ha-aretz* ("peoples of the land," Ezra 9:10-15; 10:1-5; Deut. 7). The Abrahamic covenant itself was insufficient to this end (Gen. 12:10-20; 16:1-4; 20:1-18). Apart from the Sinai covenant, Israel would have disappeared like other nations. There would be no record of an Abrahamic lineage, nor any memory of the promise God made him. This, of course, entails that the Sinai covenant was inherently temporary. It served a purpose only until the promised offspring had come. DP fails to account for this subservient role of the Sinai covenant.

If the Sinai covenant is different in kind from the Abrahamic covenant, then isn't it contrary to the Abrahamic covenant? No, "because it is not a different means of attaining the same thing" (151). "[T]he Sinai covenant was sub-eschatological. The 'life' available by that administration was only temporal life in the land of Canaan" (Deut. 16:20; 30:19) (152). In keeping with his opinion that ὁ νόμος means "*the* law" (Sinai covenant), Gordon suggests that "a law" in verse 21 should be "the law," resulting in "If the law that was given was able to make alive, then righteousness would be by the law" (151).[8]

7. Galatians 3:23–25

Thus far we have encountered Paul's use of "the promise" as synecdoche for the Abrahamic covenant and "the law" as synecdoche for the Sinai covenant. In verse 23 we are introduced to "faith" as synecdoche for the new covenant (it does not refer to the human act). "The underlying covenant-historical structure to Paul's reasoning is, I suggest, promise-law-faith . . . [H]e earlier placed Sinai as '430 years after the promise'; here he places it 'before' and 'until' faith" (155).

Based on the use of φρουρέω in 1 Corinthians 11:32, Philippians 4:7, and 1 Peter 1:5, as well as in the LXX (Josh. 6:1; Jdg. 5:1), Gordon argues that verse 23 refers to the law preserving, guarding, or protecting Israel. "The Sinai covenant, like a reversal of Jericho's gates, would not allow the Jews outside (to intermarry with the Gentiles) nor the Gentiles inside (to intermarry with the Jews)" (157). This leads him to understand παιδαγωγός (guardian) in verse 24 as serving a bodyguard role (one of the many potential roles of the broad term), rather than an instructional or disciplinary role in the individual experience of a believer (convicting them of sin). "Whatever the law-as-pedagogue did, it did it only 'before' (Πρὸ) or 'until' (εἰς, 3x) Christ, and does so 'no longer' (οὐκέτι)" (159). Thus Paul can speak favorably of the Gentile-excluding law for this purpose, but once Christ has come Paul now views it unfavorably in the same way

---

[8] Note that, with either translation, the implication is that "law" is something that can refer to more than just the Sinai covenant (either "*a* law" generally, or "*the* law *that was given*" implying the need to specify *which* law from a multitude).

that a guardian is looked upon favorably until a child has come of age, at which point it would be wrong for it to continue to act as a protective guardian.

8. Galatians 3:26–29

In light of the temporary (and now ceased) role of the Sinai covenant, "you" (Galatian Gentiles) are all sons of God through faith (v. 26). Paul contrasts how the new covenant ceremony of baptism "unites all in a common reality" while the Sinai covenant ceremonies in various ways distinguished Jew from Greek, male from female (Lev. 12:2, 4, 8; 15:19), and slave from free (Lev. 19:20; 25:39; Exod. 21:2, 20–21). In fact, Gordon argues, Mosaic law distinguished these groups specifically with regards to circumcision. Gentiles were not circumcised. Neither were females. Slaves were required to be circumcised but free sojourners or resident aliens were not.

9. Galatians 4:1–7

Chapter 4 continues and focuses the question of "Who will inherit the third reality pledged to Abraham and Sarah?" (165). Paul reiterates a similar point to 3:22–25. "[B]eing ὑπὸ νόμον was like a child being under special care and guardianship, which is necessary to the child's minority circumstance but not necessary upon the age of majority" (167). However, he adds that such a child is like a slave in regard to the question of inheritance. "We" here refers to Jews (Gentiles were never "under the law") who were kept from their inheritance (enslaved) by the elementary principles of the world until

> the work of Christ manumitted them (ἵνα τοὺς ὑπὸ νόμον ἐξαγοράσῃ) therefrom. Only then, manumitted from the covenant that separated Jew from Gentile [by the inauguration of the new covenant which terminated the Sinai covenant], could they receive their full inheritance/adoption as mature sons . . . Gentile exclusion entailed Israelite servitude and minority. (168)

10. Galatians 4:8–11

Speaking now to the Galatian Gentiles, Paul questions why they would want to be enslaved by the (previously mentioned) elementary principles of the world, which refers "to either the same *reality* or the same redemptive-historical *moment* as the season in which Israel was ὑπὸ νόμον" (168). "Now that they have come to know God (and/or be known by God), why would they observe the very covenant that had excluded them for centuries?" (169).

11. Galatians 4:21–31

Paul's allegory is not an argument *proved* from Genesis, but rather the summary of his argument *illustrated* by the Genesis narrative. He focuses on the distinction between slave and free, reiterating his argument "that life under the Sinai administration was/is a kind of bondage" (175), and the distinction of flesh and promise, reiterating the distinction between the Sinai covenant as dependent upon Israelite works and the Abrahamic covenant as dependent only on God's pledge/promise. Because Paul chose the word "promise" and "promise" is a synecdoche for the Abrahamic covenant, Paul is here comparing the Sinai covenant with the Abrahamic, not the new covenant. Furthermore,

> "Abraham had two sons" is far more likely to be a reference to two covenant administrations made with his lineage than it is a reference to one covenant (Sinai) made with his lineage and another (the new) that is plainly not made with his lineage. (175)

That said, both the Abrahamic and the new covenant embrace all nations, are characterized by faith, and are free of any threatened curse sanctions. Furthermore, the new covenant is the fulfillment of what was pledged in the Abrahamic covenant. "If we ask, then, whether the 'our mother' of 4:26 is the figurative mother of members of the Abrahamic or the new covenant, the answer is probably 'both.'" But Gordon is not quite certain.

Having said this, however, there is some good reason to think that the first-person plural here ("our mother") refers to those who are members of the new covenant . . . It is also possible that the "then/now" comparison of verse 29 also suggests that the "free son" is intended to be the new covenant believers in Paul's day. And the concluding statement in verse 31 surely suggests that it is new covenant believers who are represented by the free woman and the free child of the analogy . . . (179)

In the end, Gordon concludes that it is not necessary to make a determination because it is not critical to his covenant-historical approach to Galatians. "[W]hat is necessary for Paul is to designate the slave son as a child of Sinai" (178). Paul is referring to the Sinai covenant itself, not a misunderstanding of it. DP has characteristically misunderstood this point by thinking Paul has in mind a later perversion of the Sinai covenant, rather than the Sinai covenant delivered by the hand of Moses on Mount Sinai. "It is not two interpretations of that covenant he discusses, but 'two covenants' — one of which is specified to be the covenant made on Mount Sinai. The dominant Protestant approach has had enormous difficulty allowing Paul to speak for himself in Galatians" (176). DP "rests persistently on the notion that there is a right way and a wrong way to observe the Sinai covenant, and a right way and a wrong way to understand it" (177).

The dominant Protestant approach has routinely suggested that the reason the Sinai covenant produced children for bondage is because, as sinners, the Israelites either approached/understood the covenant the wrong way or failed to keep it because they were sinful. What the dominant Protestant approach has not explained is how/why/whether the same people did not also misunderstand the Abrahamic [or new] covenant. If the "bondage" associated with the Sinai covenant is due to human sinfulness or misunderstanding on the part of the Israelites, then why did not the same (alleged) sinfulness or misunderstanding produce bondage with the Abrahamic [or new] covenant? He refers to "two covenants" (αὗται γάρ εἰσιν δύο διαθῆκαι), only one (μία) of which produces bondage. (177)

Gordon is uncertain precisely whether the slavery associated with the Sinai covenant refers to "separation from Gentiles, its curse sanctions, or merely the frustrated aspirations regarding the third pledge to Abraham that each of these entailed (or all three)" (176), though he leans towards threatened curse sanctions. "What is unmistakable here in chapter 4, however, is that Paul regards being 'under the law' (ὑπὸ νόμον, 4:21) as being enslaved" (176).

12. Galatians 5:1

Galatians 5:1 concludes the allegory with a command not to submit to a yoke of slavery, referring to the Sinai covenant and its threatening curse sanctions (cf. Acts 15:10). "The Sinai covenant, a burdensome yoke to those who lived under it, has disappeared with the appearance of the new covenant, and Paul commanded the Galatians to submit to it no more" (180).

13. Galatians 5:2–6

Being circumcised obligates one to keep all of the Mosaic laws. "[O]ne cannot elect to observe circumcision without electing to observe other regulations, including those that segregate Israel from the Gentiles more generally" (184). Gordon notes that translators add "who would be" in "you *who would be* justified by the law," opining that it is probably not the best choice. Instead, he paraphrases:

> All who wish to obey the law yourselves, and reap whatever temporal reward you may achieve thereby in the land of Canaan, go right ahead. But Christ has nothing to do with any of that—nothing to do with temporal prosperity for one nation in Canaan, and nothing to do with the obedience by which some degree thereof might be attained. (184)

The reason for Paul's mutually exclusive distinction between Christ and the law/circumcision is because of the principle of substitution (Gal. 3:13). "Evade (if you can) the curse sanctions of Sinai by your own behavior, or evade the same through the substitutionary work of Christ. But you cannot do both; you must choose" (185). Confusingly, Gordon explains this passage by appeal to penal substitution, even quoting 3:13, yet in his previous comments on 3:13 he denied it referred to penal substitution.

Because we "wait for the hope of righteousness," verse 5 implies that "justification is itself essentially an eschatological doctrine. To be acquitted/justified in the ultimate sense is to survive God's final act of judgment that inaugurates the eschaton" (185). Paul adds the qualifier "working through love" to "indicate that 'νόμος-free' does not mean 'ethics free' or 'licentious'" (186).

14. Galatians 5:13–15

"The 'freedom' Paul refers to here is the 'freedom' from the Sinai covenant that has been his concern in his use of the ἐλευθ- group seven times (of the nine in Galatians) from 4:22 until here" (189). Yet Paul is not therefore a proponent of licentiousness. Gordon does not elaborate on Paul's quotation of Leviticus 19:8 but suggests Paul quotes it because his audience finds the text authoritative, not necessarily because he does.

15. Galatians 5:16–24

"Consistently with his reasoning in chapter 3, he places νόμος in the pre-eschatological era and πνεῦμα in the eschatological era: 'If (since) you are led by the Spirit, you are not under the law'" (192). Paul tailors his recurring list of "works of the flesh" and "fruit of the Spirit" to address the divisive nature of the situation in Galatia.

16. Galatians 6:1–5

"The law of Christ" (τὸν νόμον τοῦ Χριστοῦ) does not mean "the Mosaic law as interpreted by Christ," because "Paul can 'do ethics,' as it were, entirely without the Mosaic law." Paul more likely means "The important thing now is to live as followers of Christ, following the stipulations of his covenant; if we need a νόμον now, it is Christ's law" (196). In a footnote, Gordon mentions the distinction between "the law in the hand of Moses" view (which sees Paul citing portions of the Decalogue because the Decalogue itself is obligatory to Christians) and "the law in the hand of Christ" view (which sees Paul quoting the Decalogue because it reflects the creational duty of the *imitatio Dei*). He says he embraces the latter view and quotes John Gill's *The Law in the Hand of Christ: A Sermon Preached May 24, 1761, at Broad-Mead, in Bristol*.[9]

17. Galatians 6:11–16

Paul's mention of "the Israel of God" is deliberate and surprising. "God of Israel" appears over one hundred times in the OT, but never "Israel of God." Paul refers not to Abraham's ethnic descendants but "to 'Israel' as the true inheritors of the promises made to Abraham (3:29; 4:28; and to the nations through his single descendant, 3:14, 16), to 'Israel' as the true people of God, and to 'Israel' as those who have the faith of Abraham (Gal. 3:7)" (202).

---

[9] It is worth noting that Gordon self-consciously identifies himself with the subservient covenant tradition, earlier citing Samuel Bolton. John Gill held to a form of the subservient covenant view as well. For an excellent analysis of the tradition, see Samuel D. Renihan *From Shadow to Substance: The Federal Theology of the English Particular Baptist Baptists (1642–1704)* (Oxford, UK: Regent's Park College, 2018). Regarding the law of Moses, note Richard C. Barcellos *In Defense of the Decalogue* (Enumclaw, WA: Winepress Publishing, 2001), 61, where he says: "Hearty agreement must be given when New Covenant theologians argue for the abolition of the Old Covenant. This is clearly the teaching of the Old and New Testaments (see Jeremiah 31:31-32; Second Corinthians 3; Galatians 3, 4; Ephesians 2:14-15; Hebrews 8-10). The whole law of Moses, *as it functioned under the Old Covenant*, has been abolished, including the Ten Commandments. Not one jot or tittle of the law of Moses functions *as Old Covenant law* anymore and to act as if it does constitutes redemptive-historical retreat and neo-Judaizing. However, to acknowledge that the law of Moses no longer functions as *Old Covenant law* is not to accept that it no longer functions; it simply no longer functions *as Old Covenant law*. This can be seen by the fact that the New Testament teaches *both* the abrogation of the law of the Old Covenant *and* its abiding moral validity under the New Covenant." See also Richard C. Barcellos "John Owen and New Covenant Theology: Owen on the Old and New Covenants and the Functions of the Decalogue in Redemptive History in Historical and Contemporary Perspective," in *Covenant Theology: From Adam to Christ*, ed. Ronald D. Miller, James M. Renihan, and Francisco Orozco (Palmdale, CA: Reformed Baptist Academic Press, 2005), 317. Compare with Martin Luther, "How Christians Should Regard Moses," trans. and ed. by E. Theodore Bachmann, *Luther's Works: Word and Sacrament I*, vol. 35 (Philadelphia: Muhlenberg Press, 1960), 161–174.

Analysis

Promise, Law, Faith is an exciting volume simply because Gordon approaches the text of Galatians from a covenant theology perspective known historically as the subservient covenant tradition, which views the Sinai covenant neither as the Adamic covenant of works, nor the covenant of grace, but a distinct third covenant that was subservient to the covenant of grace. Gordon quotes Samuel Bolton as representative of his own view.

> It was given by way of subserviency to the Gospel and a fuller revelation of the covenant of grace; it was temporary, and had respect to Canaan and God's blessing there, if and as Israel obeyed. It had no relation to heaven, for that was promised by another covenant which God made before He entered the subservient covenant. This is the opinion which I myself desire modestly to propound, for I have not been convinced that it is injurious to holiness or disagreeable to the mind of God in Scripture.[10]

The majority view of the sixteenth and seventeenth centuries held that the Sinai covenant was the covenant of grace (in substance).[11]

---

[10] Samuel Bolton, *The True Bounds of Christian Freedom* (reprint, Edinburgh: Banner of Truth Trust, 1964), 99. Quoted in Gordon, 39, n. 25. Compare with Augustine, *A Work on the Proceedings of Pelagius,* trans. Peter Holmes, Robert Ernest Wallis, Benjamin B. Warfield, vol. 5 of *A Select Library of the Nicene and Post-Nicene Fathers of the Christian Church,* ed. Philip Schaff (Grand Rapids: WM. B. Eerdmans Publishing Company), 189, where he says: "In that testament, however, which is properly called the Old, and was given on Mount Sinai, only earthly happiness is expressly promised . . . And these, indeed, are figures of the spiritual blessings which appertain to the New Testament."

[11] WCF 7.4–6. See John Calvin, *Commentaries on the Book of the Prophet Jeremiah and the Lamentations,* trans. John Owen (Grand Rapids: Christian Classica Ethereal Library), Jer. 31:31–32. "Now, as to the *new* covenant, it is not so called, because it is contrary to the first covenant; for God is never inconsistent with himself, nor is he unlike himself, he then who once made a covenant with his chosen people, had not changed his purpose, as though he had forgotten his faithfulness. It then follows, that the first covenant was inviolable; besides, he had already made his covenant with Abraham, and the Law was a confirmation of that covenant. As then the Law depended on that covenant which God made with his servant Abraham, it follows that God could never have made a new, that is, a contrary or a different covenant . . . These things no doubt sufficiently shew that God has never made any other covenant

This is foundational to what Gordon calls the DP reading of Galatians, which is anchored by the belief that Paul's negative statements about the law do not refer to the gracious Sinai covenant itself, but rather to a misunderstanding and abuse of Mosaic law. The Judaizers abstracted the law from its gracious covenant context, therefore Paul's statements are about the bare law itself apart from the Sinai covenant.

The 2016 Orthodox Presbyterian Church General Assembly report on republication commended this view as consistent with the Westminster Confession, while denying the subservient interpretation was. It commended the "misinterpretation principle" defined as "the notion that Paul, in texts such as Gal 3 and Rom. 10:4–5, is refuting a Jewish misinterpretation of the law (namely, that the Mosaic law contained a substantial republication of the covenant of works)."[12] It further clarified that "misinterpretive republication" refers to

> the idea that the covenant of works is not actually republished in a substantial sense in the Mosaic covenant but is present only in the misunderstanding of those who opposed Paul's teaching of a substantially gracious Mosaic covenant. Hence, the language of contrast between the Abrahamic and Mosaic covenants rests in the minds of Paul's opponents, but not in Paul's actual theology.[13]

---

than that which he made formerly with Abraham, and at length confirmed by the hand of Moses. This subject might be more fully handled; but it is enough briefly to shew, that the covenant which God made at first is perpetual."

[12] *Report of the Committee to Study Republication Presented to the Eighty-third (2016) General Assembly of the Orthodox Presbyterian Church*, 91. Available at https://www.opc.org/GA/republication.html. Accessed 1 October 2020. The report is commendable notably for its accurate representation of the Westminster Confession's view and for recognizing the subservient covenant view was self-consciously distinct from it and mutually exclusive to it. That said, the Report does not adequately represent or engage with the subservient covenant view and it mistakenly claims Owen held that the Mosaic was in substance the covenant of works promising eternal life. Rather, Owen held to the subservient covenant view. See Renihan *From Shadow to Substance*, 195–223.

[13] *Report of the Committee to Study Republication*, 91. Note well: If in the texts in question the covenant of works "is present only in the misunderstanding of those who opposed Paul's teaching," then, as John Murray realized, "[i]n connection with the promise of life it does not appear justifiable to appeal, as frequently has been done, to the principle enunciated in certain texts (cf. Lev. 18:5; Rom. 10:5; Gal. 3:12), 'This do and thou shalt live'." That is why Murray rejected the covenant *of works*. (It could be argued that he still held to an Adamic covenant but simply called it the

I believe the Westminster Confession's understanding of the Sinai covenant is incorrect, thus I welcome Gordon's contribution to understanding the letter of Galatians from a more biblical understanding of the covenants. However, I believe he has swung the pendulum too far in the opposite direction. I also believe his understanding of the covenants may be refined yet further to be even more biblical.

1. The tripartite Abrahamic covenant

Gordon's understanding of the Abrahamic, Sinai, and new covenants as three distinct covenants (rather than three phases or "administrations" of the same covenant) is an excellent starting place. He correctly notes:

> Within the Hebrew Bible there are several covenants . . . Each of these covenants has its own integrity and its own purpose. They cannot and do not meld into one another regarding their parties, their stipulations, or their benefits. (54)[14]

Gordon very helpfully distributes the Abrahamic covenant into three distinct promises: to become numerous, to inherit the land of Canaan, and to bless all the nations of the world.[15] He also correctly recognizes

---

"Adamic Administration," yet even then he precisely rejected the works component of such an arrangement. "Adam could claim the fulfilment of the promise if he stood the probation, but only on the basis of God's faithfulness, not on the basis of justice." See John Murray, "The Adamic Administration" in *Collected Writings*, vol. II (Edinburgh; Carlisle, PA: Banner of Truth Trust, 1977), 47–60.

[14] Insofar as the "substance" of a covenant refers to its Aristotelian essence, it is determined by the covenant's parties, stipulations and benefits. See *Report of the Committee to Study Republication*, 11. Note that the WCF conflates the Aristotelian substance/accidents distinction with the Pauline substance/shadows distinction at 7.6.

[15] Here I agree with Gordon and disagree with Nehemiah Coxe, who saw the third promise as part of the new covenant, properly speaking, and only mentioned or declared in the midst of the Covenant of Circumcision. Coxe believed that being the father of the Messiah (*historia salutis*) was a special privilege Abraham received as part of the new covenant, whereas I believe it was a promise of the Abrahamic Covenant itself. See Nehemiah Coxe, "A Discourse of the Covenants that God made with men before the Law," in *Covenant Theology: From Adam to Christ*, 72, 74, 75, 78, 80.

that the first two were fulfilled prior to Christ. Galatians 3:8 "expressly refers to the third (prior to Paul, unfulfilled) aspect of the tripartite pledge God made to Abraham, to bless the nations/Gentiles through him. The other two parts, becoming numerous and inheriting the land, had been fulfilled many years before." (109). I do not believe, however, he draws the necessary conclusions from this distinction for his study of Galatians. His understanding of Paul's use of synecdoche leads him to interpret "promise" as referring to the whole Abrahamic covenant, rather than just part of it and thus interpret Paul as "contrast[ing] the Abrahamic covenant with the Sinai covenant in five ways" (121). But if 3:8 "expressly refers to the third" promise, in distinction from the other two, then perhaps the same is true throughout the rest of the letter. Recall above that Gordon said in verse 14 "Paul is referring here *and throughout Galatians* to the third pledge God made to Abraham: that through Abraham's seed, all nations/families of the earth would be 'blessed'" (130, emphasis added). If this is the case, then in the same way that Gordon uses 3:17 as an interpretative foundation for understanding ὁ νόμος throughout the letter, perhaps 3:8 should serve as an interpretative foundation for understanding ἐπαγγελίαν (promise) throughout the letter.

Again in 3:16 Gordon recognizes that ἐπαγγελίαν refers not to the Abrahamic covenant as a whole, but to the third promise specifically. He argued that Paul understood the "seed" of the first two promises to be corporate, but the implications of this acknowledgment remain untapped by Gordon. Paul is not merely arguing that the third promise refers to a singular seed. He is arguing that it refers to a singular seed *in distinction from the other two Abrahamic promises*, which refer to a corporate seed. Paul is making an intra-Abrahamic argument. As mentioned above, Alexander argues that the grammar of Genesis 22:17b indicates that it should be translated "And your offspring will possess the gate of his (not 'their') enemies," a reading that is confirmed by Psalm 72:17b. He concludes "the 'seed' mentioned in Genesis 22:17b-18a does not refer to all Abraham's descendants, but rather to a single individual."[16] Collins builds upon this, pointing out that Paul's quotation in Galatians 3:8 is a composite of different Genesis texts, including 22:18, which makes perfect sense

---

[16] Alexander, "Further Observations on the Term 'Seed' in Genesis," 365.

of Paul's hitherto perplexing argumentation in Galatians 3:16. Paul is not making a typological or *sensus plenior* argument from the text of Genesis (which does not comport with his insistence on the grammar of the promise). "[W]e should give more room to the possibility that he saw things that are really there —things that we have not yet found."[17] John Brown actually made the same argument in 1853.

> It is just as if he had said, 'In the passage I refer to, the word *seed* is used of an individual, just as when it is employed of Seth, Gen. iv. 25, where he is called "another seed," and said to be given in the room of Abel, whom Cain slew. In looking carefully at the promise recorded, Gen. xxii. 16–18, the phrase *"seed"* seems used with a different reference in the two parts of the promise—the first part of the 17th verse plainly referring to a class of descendants; the last clause and the 18th verse to an individual, and that individual is Christ.'[18]

Yet others have objected that Paul cannot be quoting Genesis 22:18 because that text does not contain καὶ ("and to") whereas Paul's quotation does ("and to your offspring").[19] Therefore Paul must be referring to Genesis 13:15 and/or 17:8, which Paul interprets typologically or spiritually. Collins argues this does not matter because Paul is merely alluding to 22:18 (and 3:8 is a composite). While this is somewhat true, I think a stronger point is that Paul is making an intra-Abrahamic argument contrasting the different promises by comparing the seed to whom they refer. Paul acknowledges that the first two promises, particularly the land promise, were made to Abraham's carnal offspring. "I will give *to you and your offspring* after you the land" (Gen. 17:8; 13:15). But 22:18 (the specific promise to which Paul has been referring since 3:8) "does not say, 'And to offsprings,' referring to many, but referring to one, 'And

---

[17] Collins, "Galatians 3:16: What Kind of Exegete was Paul?" 86.

[18] John Brown, *An Exposition of the Epistle of Paul the Apostle to the Galatians* (Edinburgh/London/New York: William Oliphant and Sons, 1853), 144. I was directed to this reference by an anonymous Twitter account, challenging the view that Twitter is good for nothing.

[19] J. B. Lightfoot, *St. Paul's Epistle to the Galatians* (1865; reprint, Lynn, MA: Hendrickson, 1981), 142, says "καὶ must be part of the quotation. These considerations restrict the reference to Gen. xiii.15, xvii.8."

to your offspring" (Gal. 3:16). Thus, the promise to bless all nations in Abraham's offspring does *not* refer to the Jews, even though the promise of the land *did*, and therefore it is not a requirement that one *live like a Jew* in order to receive that promised blessing (unlike the land promise, which did require circumcision; Josh. 5:1-12; Gen. 17:14; Exod. 4:24-26). In other words, Paul is expounding upon the dichotomous nature of the Abrahamic covenant.[20]

In light of this, it must be observed that with regard to the promises there are three, and only three, offspring of Abraham: his numerous carnal offspring, his singular, Messianic carnal offspring, and his spiritual offspring (all those united to Christ). The offspring of those united to Christ are not Abraham's offspring. None of the Abrahamic promises were to them.[21]

---

[20] Gordon's tripartite division has been simplified by others into a bipartite division distinguished by the seed. Augustine, *City of God*, trans. Marcus Dods, vol. 2 of *A Select Library of the Nicene and Post-Nicene Fathers of the Christian Church*, ed. Philip Schaff (Grand Rapids: WM. B. Eerdmans Publishing Company), XVI.16, says: "Now it is to be observed that two things are promised to Abraham, the one, that his seed should possess the land of Canaan, which is intimated when it is said, 'Go into a land that I will show thee, and I will make of thee a great nation;' but the other far more excellent, not about the carnal but the spiritual seed, through which he is the father, not of the one Israelite nation, but of all nations who follow the footprints of his faith, which was first promised in these words, 'And in thee shall all tribes of the earth be blessed.'" John Owen, "Exercitation 6. Oneness of the Church," *An Exposition of the Epistle to the Hebrews: Introduction*, vol. 17 of *The Works of John Owen*, ed. William H. Goold (Albany, OR: Books for the Ages, 2000), 177, says: "Two privileges did God grant unto Abraham, upon his separation to a special interest in the old promise and covenant . . . Answerably unto this twofold end of the separation of Abraham, there was a double seed allotted unto him; — a seed according to the flesh, separated to the bringing forth of the Messiah according unto the flesh; and a seed according to the promise, that is, such as by faith should have interest in the promise, or all the elect of God."

[21] Many mistakenly put themselves in the place of Abraham and claim that God promised to be a God to their offspring. They forget their place as Abraham's offspring, not Abraham himself. Genesis 17:7-8 refers to Abraham's offspring down through the generations, not just his immediate offspring. It was fulfilled when God redeemed Israel out of Egypt, gave them the land of Canaan, established the old covenant with them, and dwelt in their midst (Exod. 6:7; 19:4-6; 29:45; Deut. 4:32-40; 26:16-19; 29:10-13; Amos 3:1-2; Hos. 1:9). That is, the promise was sub-eschatological. Gordon notes this in another essay "Murray (and his followers) implicitly believe that the only *relation* God sustains to people is that of Redeemer (which, by my light, is not a relation but an office). I would argue, by contrast, that God was just as surely

2. The Abrahamic covenant vs. the Sinai covenant

If Paul is expounding upon the dichotomous nature of the Abrahamic covenant, then it does not seem appropriate to interpret Paul as comparing the Sinai covenant with the Abrahamic covenant *simpliciter*, as Gordon does. He offers the following table as a summary of Paul's comparison between the two covenants in Galatians 3:6–14.

Abrahamic Covenant	Sinai Covenant
"those who are characterized by faith"	"those who are characterized by works of the law"
Includes the nations	Excludes the nations
Blesses	Curses
Justifies	Justifies no one
Promise	Law

Let us examine each of these comparisons to see if they hold up.

3. Promise vs. law

The last comparison (promise vs. law) Gordon derives from 3:17–18, which he interprets to be a statement regarding the contradictory *natures* of the two covenants: promise inheritance vs. law inheritance.

> ὁ νόμος is not and cannot be an alternative way of arriving at the blessings associated with the Abrahamic covenant . . . The specific reason the law does not annul/de-ratify the Abrahamic promise is that if it were an alternative means of arriving at that promise it would "make the promise void. For if the inheritance comes by the

---

Israel's God when He *cursed* the nation as when He *blessed* it. His pledge to be Israel's God, via the terms of the Sinai administration, committed him to curse Israel for disobedience just as much as to bless her for obedience. In being Israel's God, he sustained the relation of covenant suzerain to her; he did not bless or curse any other nation for its covenant fidelity or infidelity. In this sense, he was *not* the God of other nations as he was the God of Israel" (T. David Gordon, "Reflections on Auburn Theology," in *By Faith Alone: Answering the Challenges to the Doctrine of Justification*, ed. Gary L. W. Johnson, Guy P. Waters (Wheaton, IL: Crossway Books, 2006), 120).

law, it no longer comes by promise; but God gave it to Abraham by a promise." The law, with over six hundred commands, cannot become the means to attaining that which was promised to Abraham without voiding its promissory nature altogether. The law, whose recipients live under the threatened curse sanction, cannot be the means of inheriting the blessings that were promised to Abraham without corrupting entirely what "promise" means . . . *Four times in three verses (3:16–18), Paul employs the language of "promise," because the Abrahamic covenant (which came 430 years earlier than the Sinai covenant) was and is essentially promissory.* (140, emphasis added)

Does Paul employ the language of "promise" because the type of covenant God made with Abraham was a promissory covenant? Or does Paul employ the language of "promise" because he is referring to a specific promise, the one mentioned in 3:8? Gordon notes that when νόμος is anarthrous, translators must choose to add either "a" or "the" (*a* law, *the* law). He argues (in verse 21 specifically) that νόμος should always be translated "the law" because Paul is referring specifically to the Sinai covenant, not to a general or abstract concept of law. I believe a similar situation occurs in verse 18 regarding the translation of ἐπαγγελίας. Most translations end verse 17 with a particular reference ("*the* promise"), yet they translate ἐπαγγελίας as a general reference in verse 18 ("*a* promise"), so as to suggest Paul is making a comparison between two different ways of inheriting something in general (inheriting something by promise is read as synonymous with inheriting something by grace, cf. Rom 4:4; 11:16).[22] I believe the NET translation makes more sense: "For if the inheritance is based on the law, it is no longer based on the promise, but God graciously gave it to Abraham through the promise."[23] Rather than making a general point about what type of covenant the Abrahamic is (after all, every covenant is based on promise, even a covenant of works[24]), Paul is reiterating the point he made in 2:21. If

---

[22] See Meredith G. Kline, *By Oath Consigned: A Reinterpretation of the Covenant Signs of Circumcision and Baptism* (Grand Rapids, MI: Eerdmans, 1968), 23–24.

[23] NET Bible. https://netbible.com/copyright/. Accessed 1 October 2020.

[24] What matters is the specifics of the promise. John Owen, *An Exposition of the Epistle to the Hebrews: Hebrews 8:1-10:39*, vol. 22 of *The Works of John Owen*, ed. William H. Goold (Albany, OR: Books for the Ages, 2000), 79–82, says: "[E]very covenant between God and man must be founded on and resolved into 'promises.'... It is

the inheritance is based on the law, it is no longer based on Christ, but God gave it to Abraham through *the promise of Christ* (3:8).[25]

4. Includes vs. excludes the nations

Gordon argues that the Abrahamic covenant includes the nations while the Sinai covenant excludes the nations. In light of the above distinctions, is that accurate? Did the first two Abrahamic promises include the nations? Was the land of Canaan promised to the nations or only to Abraham's carnal offspring? The fulfillment of the land promise entailed the expulsion of the Gentiles (Exod. 23:31; 33:1–2; Deut. 7:17–24; Acts 13:19). Thus, the inclusion and exclusion of the nations points to an Abrahamic dichotomy, rather than an Abrahamic contrast with the Sinai covenant because the first two Abrahamic promises exclude the nations while the third includes the nations.

5. Blesses vs. curses

Is it true that the Abrahamic covenant blessed while the Sinai covenant cursed? Genesis 12:3 declares a curse upon all who oppose Abraham and his descendants, which specifically refers to the nations, Israel's enemies (Num. 24:8–9). It may be rightly pointed out that this curse was upon those *outside* of the Abrahamic covenant, but what of Genesis 17:14? There God declares that any member of the Abrahamic covenant who is not circumcised will be put to death, a curse Moses himself nearly came under (Exod. 4:27; see meaning of "cut off" in

---

necessary from the nature of a covenant... And herein lies the great difference between the promises of the *covenant of works* and those of the *covenant of grace*... And this is the first thing that was to be declared, namely, that every divine covenant is established on promises." The covenant of works was based on a promise in that it "promised life upon the fulfilling [of the law]" (WCF/2LCF 19.1).

[25] In *The Commentary and Homilies of St. John Chrysostom, Archbishop of Constantinople, on the Epistles of St. Paul the Apostle to the Galatians and Ephesians*, trans. Gross Alexander, vol. 13 of *A Select Library of the Nicene and Post-Nicene Fathers of the Christian Church*, ed. Philip Schaff (Grand Rapids: WM. B. Eerdmans Publishing Company), 28, Chrysostom says: "It was promised Abraham that by his seed the heathen should be blessed; and his seed according to the flesh is Christ; four hundred and thirty years after came the Law; now, if the Law bestows the blessings even life and righteousness, that promise is annulled."

Lev. 23:29–30; Num. 15:30–36; Exod. 31:14–15). Surely this amounts to a *threatened* curse — the kind Gordon is at pains to attribute to the Sinai covenant. It is not accurate to say, "Abraham's covenant threatened with no curses at all" (115). Thus, blessing and curse does not appear to distinguish the Abrahamic covenant from the Sinai covenant.

6. "Of faith" vs. "of works"

Paul says the Sinai covenant is "of works," which Gordon understands to mean "If they would obey (i.e., do what he commanded), then God would bless them in the land of Canaan; and if they would not obey (do contrary to what he commanded), then God would curse them there" (124). This is in contrast to the inheritance of the third Abrahamic promise, which is "of faith." But what of the other promises? Did Abraham's offspring inherit the land of Canaan through faith apart from works of the law or through works of the law? Scripture is clear that obedience to the Sinai covenant was a condition of Israel's entrance into the promised land (Exod. 19:5–8; 23:20–22; Deut. 4:1; 6:3, 17–18, 24–25; 7:12; 8:1–2; 11:8, 22–24; 29:13; Jer. 11:5). Israel entered into the Sinai covenant in the wilderness prior to entering the land. As Gordon notes in a prior essay "While the land was eventually given to the Israelites, the terms of the Sinai covenant delayed their inheritance by forty years . . ."[26]

---

[26] T. David Gordon, "Abraham and Sinai Contrasted in Galatians 3:6–14," in *The Law is Not of Faith: Essays on Works and Grace in the Mosaic Covenant,* ed. Bryan D. Estelle, J.V. Fesko, David VanDrunen (Phillipsburg, NJ: P&R Publishing, 2009), 247. See also Dennis E. Johnson, *Him We Proclaim: Preaching Christ from All the Scriptures* (Phillipsburg, NJ: P&R Publishing, 2007), 298, "On the other hand it also is true to say that Israel, though small and stubborn, is receiving the land through obedience. Moses has already drawn a connection between obedience and conquest of the Promised Land in Deuteronomy 4:1. 'And now, O Israel, listen to the statutes and the rules that I am teaching you, and do them, that you may live, and go in and take possession of the land that the Lord, the God of your fathers, is giving you.' Israel is to hear and to do the Lord's commands 'that' the promised consequences might follow, namely life and possession of the land. Israel's reception of the relative and temporal/temporary possession of life and land as a reward for relative fidelity to the law of the Lord foreshadows a covenantal principle of reciprocity that the apostle Paul will articulate in its eschatologized, absolutized form: 'The one who does [God's commands] shall live by them.' (Gal 3:12)."

Israel did not inherit the promised land until the disobedient generation died in the wilderness and the second generation subsequently obeyed (Deut. 8:2).[27] Thus being "of works" or "of faith" does not distinguish the Abrahamic covenant from the Sinai covenant, though it does distinguish the different inheritances promised in the dichotomous Abrahamic covenant.

All of this brings us to the big elephant in the room: circumcision is Abrahamic. Gordon recognizes that circumcision separates Jew and Gentile. It did this from its inception, not 430 years later (Gen. 34:15). Circumcision is just as Abrahamic as it is Mosaic, which is why Scripture calls the Abrahamic covenant the covenant of circumcision (Acts 7:8). This alone negates the idea that Paul's argument is to distinguish the Abrahamic covenant (*simpliciter*) from the Sinai covenant. Whatever incompatibility Paul finds between circumcision and the new covenant, he finds between the covenant of circumcision and the new covenant. The Sinai covenant did not change the meaning of circumcision.[28] The DP interpretation argues, at this point,

---

[27] See Bryan D. Estelle, "Leviticus 18:5 and Deuteronomy 30:1–14 in Biblical Theological Development: Entitlement to Heaven Foreclosed and Proffered," in *The Law is Not of Faith*, 118, n. 45. "[I]n the context of the Old Testament itself, there is often the assumption that the law can be kept in some measure and indeed has been kept by certain generations, such as the generation of Joshua and Caleb." Deut. 9:4–6 would appear to contradict this interpretation. That passage, however, is not directed specifically at the second generation, but at Israel collectively, inclusive of the first, disobedient generation (cp. Deut 3:26; 4:21). God was humbling the second generation, reminding them they were only spared their parents' destruction by his mercy.

[28] Circumcision was not a sign or seal of Abraham's (or anyone else's) faith in the *ordo salutis*. As a sign, it dedicated all recipients to the service of Yahweh and obligated them to keep the whole law. See John D. Meade, "Circumcision of Flesh to Circumcision of Heart: The Typology of the Sign of the Abrahamic Covenant," in *Progressive Covenantalism*, ed. Stephen J. Wellum, Brent E. Parker (Nashville, TN: B&H Academic, 2016), 127–58 (note that Meade's unwillingness to identify biblical-theological "heart circumcision" with systematic-theological "regeneration" such that individuals in the OT were regenerate but not circumcised of heart represents a primary difference between Progressive Covenantalism and 1689 Federalism). As a seal, it guaranteed that the Abrahamic promises (notably the third) would be fulfilled (*historia salutis*). The Appendix to the 2LCF quotes John Lightfoot's translation of Rom. 4:11. "Circumcision is nothing, if we respect the time, for now it was without use, that end of it being especially fulfilled; for which it had been instituted: this end the Apostle declares in these words, Rom. 4.11 . But I fear that by most translations

that Paul is not addressing a proper understanding of circumcision, but a misunderstanding and misuse of circumcision. But Gordon (rightly) rejects that line of reasoning.

Likewise, the Sinai covenant did not change the condition of Israel's inheritance of the promised land (after all, once a covenant is ratified it cannot be annulled or voided). Circumcision obligated the one circumcised to keep the whole law (Gal. 5:3) even pre-Sinai to the extent that it was known. Recall that an offspring of Abraham would be cut off (killed) for trying to opt out of this obligation (Gen. 17:14; Exod. 4:24-26), and you begin to see why Peter says circumcision was a yoke "neither our fathers nor we have been able to bear" (Acts 15:10). The best way to understand the relationship between the Abrahamic covenant and the Sinai covenant, I suggest, is that the latter served as an addendum to the former, elaborating upon the obedience required by Abraham's carnal offspring inherent in the original covenant of circumcision.

7. Justifies vs. does not justify

Gordon's final contrast between the Abrahamic covenant and the Sinai covenant is that the former justifies while the latter does not. He

---

they are not sufficiently suited to the end of circumcision, and the scope of the Apostle whilst something of their own is by them inserted . . . as if circumcision was given to Abraham for a Seal of that Righteousness which he had being yet uncircumcised, which we will not deny to be in some sense true, but we believe that circumcision had chiefly a far different respect. Give me leave thus to render the words; *And he received the sign of circumcision, a seal of the Righteousness of Faith, which was to be in the uncircumcision,* Which *was to be* (I say) not *which had been*, not that which Abraham had whilst he was yet uncircumcised; but that which his uncircumcised seed should have, that is the Gentiles, who in time to come should imitate the faith of Abraham." (The Appendix cites this as Hor. Hebrai, on the I Cor. 7. 19. p.42, 43.) Note also John Brown, *An Exposition of the Epistle of Paul the Apostle to the Galatians*, 142, where he says: "God had, in the case of Abraham, showed that justification is by believing; He had, in the revelation made to Abraham, declared materially that justification by faith was to come upon the Gentiles. This arrangement was confirmed or ratified, both by circumcision, which the apostle tells us was 'the seal of justification by faith,' and by the solemn promise made to Abraham that, 'in him,' along with him, in the same way as he was, 'all nations should be blessed.'"

appears to assume this point based on Galatians 3:6, as it is not a point he demonstrates. Abraham was justified; therefore, the Abrahamic covenant justifies. This assumption, however, is negated by Gordon's (correct) understanding that "justification is itself essentially an eschatological doctrine. To be acquitted/justified in the ultimate sense is to survive God's final act of judgment that inaugurates the eschaton" (185). Gordon refers to "making alive" and "acquittal/righteousness" (3:21) as "two realities of the eschaton" (151). He recognizes that the promised Spirit, received by Jew and Gentile in Paul's day, is an eschatological gift. A key component of his covenant-historical interpretation, however, is that "The Sinai covenant (ὁ νόμος) governed God's visible people on earth *before* the eschatological age. It was associated, temporally, with sin and the flesh, with the pre-eschatological order" (107). He says, "The eschatological ('promised') Spirit will not come upon the Jews until that day when the eschatological blessings come to the Gentiles" (130). If "the Spirit is the active agent who produces faith in Jew and Gentile alike" (130), and that Spirit does not come until Christ, then how could anyone prior to Christ be saved? How could Abraham have received the future-promised Spirit through faith "just as" (3:6) the Galatian Gentiles did? How could Abraham be justified by the Abrahamic covenant if in the course of history the Abrahamic covenant is just as pre-eschatological as the Sinai covenant? One cannot say the Abrahamic covenant justified without rejecting the *historia testamentorum*. "Until and unless we think covenant-historically, we cannot think Paul's thoughts after him . . . His 'whens' (4:3, 3, 8), 'befores' (3:23), 'afters/nows' (3:17, 25; 4:9), and 'untils' (3:19) must become ours" (212). The eschatological gifts of the Spirit, faith, making alive, and justification can only come from an eschatological covenant and "the new covenant is profoundly and pervasively eschatological" (9). Wrestling with a similar dilemma in Hebrews 8:10, Calvin says, "There is yet no reason why God should not have extended the grace of the new covenant to the fathers. This is the true solution of the question."[29] Thus justification is not a contrast

---

[29] John Calvin, *Commentaries on the Epistle of Paul the Apostle to the Hebrews*, trans. John Owen (Grand Rapids: Christian Classica Ethereal Library), Heb. 8:10. Calvin likely gleaned this solution from Augustine who made many similar comments.

between the Abrahamic covenant and the Sinai covenant, but between the new covenant and both the Abrahamic and Sinai covenants.[30]

Augustine, *A Work on the Proceedings of Pelagius*, 189, says: "[T]he happy persons, who even in that early age [the Old Testament] were by the grace of God taught to understand the distinction now set forth, were thereby made the children of promise, and were accounted in the secret purpose of God as heirs of the New Testament; although they continued with perfect fitness to administer the Old Testament to the ancient people of God." In Augustine, *A Treatise Against Two Letters of the Pelagians,* trans. Peter Holmes, Robert Ernest Wallis, Benjamin B. Warfield, vol. 5 of *A Select Library of the Nicene and Post-Nicene Fathers of the Christian Church*, ed. Philip Schaff (Grand Rapids: WM. B. Eerdmans Publishing Company), III.11–12, 406–07, he says: "These pertain to the new testament [covenant], are the children of promise, and are regenerated by God the Father and a free mother. Of this kind were all the righteous men of old, and Moses himself, the minister of the old testament, the heir of the new . . . Let us, therefore, choose whether to call the righteous men of old the children of the bondwoman or of the free. Be it far from us to say, of the bondwoman; therefore if of the free, they pertain to the new testament [covenant] in the Holy Spirit, whom, as making alive, the apostle opposes to the killing letter. For on what ground do they not belong to the grace of the new testament [covenant?]." See also Joshua N. Moon, *Jeremiah's New Covenant: An Augustinian Reading* (University Park, PA: The Pennsylvania State University Press, 2011). John Frame recognizes this as well in John Frame, *Systematic Theology: An Introduction to Christian Belief* (Phillipsburg, NJ: P&R Publishing, 2013) 79–81, where he says: "Everyone who has ever been saved has been saved through the new covenant in Christ . . . [T]he efficacy of the New Covenant, unlike that of previous covenants, extends to God's elect prior to Jesus' atonement. When believers in the Old Testament experienced 'circumcision of the heart,' or when they were Jews 'inwardly,' they were partaking of the power of the New Covenant." And Michael Horton says similar in Michael Horton, *Rediscovering the Holy Spirit,* (Grand Rapids: Zondervan, 2017), 152, where he says: "There are clear passages indicating that 'the forgiveness of sins' is unique to the New Covenant ('remember their sins no more'; Jer 31:34) . . . Kuyper seems to confirm this conclusion. He argued that the energies of the Spirit at Pentecost worked retroactively in the lives of OT saints." See also Coxe, *A Discourse on the Divine Covenants,* 75, where he says: "The grace and blessings of the new covenant were given and ensured to Abraham for himself."

[30] The Abrahamic covenant of circumcision does promise that the nations will be blessed (referring to justification by faith), but this promise is of a *historia salutis* nature, not an *ordo salutis* nature. It promises that *Abraham will be the father of the seed of the woman* who will one day bless the nations (by establishing the new covenant, which bestows the *ordo salutis* blessings of the Spirit and forgiveness of sins; Deut. 30:6; Heb. 8:6–13). See John Owen, *An Exposition of the Epistle to the Hebrews: Hebrews 8:1–10:39,* 90, where he says: "[T]his covenant with Abraham was with respect to other things [than the *ordo salutis* covenant of grace], especially the proceeding of the promised Seed from his loins." See also John Owen, *The Oneness of the Church,* 177,

This helps resolve Gordon's dilemma of how to interpret Paul's allegory in Galatians 4:21–31. Is Paul comparing the Abrahamic and Sinai covenant, or the Sinai and new covenant? As Gordon noted, all the textual indicators point to Paul comparing Sinai to the new covenant. His reasons for considering it a comparison between the Abrahamic and Sinai covenants are those addressed above, as well as his opinion that "'Abraham had two sons' is far more likely to be a reference to two covenant administrations made with his lineage" (175). This seems an odd line of thought given that Paul's entire argument has been to demonstrate that those who are of faith (the new covenant) are Abraham's sons. Furthermore, Gordon is being overly literal in his reading of the allegory on this point (for example, Paul is not arguing that a covenant was made with Ishmael) and missing the typological significance Paul gives Isaac and Ishmael. As Günther H. Juncker notes, "As a child of promise whose birth was wholly dependent on the gracious activity of God, Isaac stands as a type of the 'children of promise,' namely, Jewish and Gentile believers."[31] Paul's point is to illustrate how the Abrahamic covenant gave birth to two different, subsequent covenants (Sinai and new). Commenting on this passage, Augustine notes, "This interpretation of the passage, handed down to us with apostolic authority, shows how we ought to understand the Scriptures of the two covenants—the old

---

where he says: "[God promised Abraham] [t]hat according to the flesh he should be the father of the Messiah, the promised seed . . . In pursuit hereof were his posterity separated from the rest of the world, and preserved a peculiar people, that through them the promised Seed might be brought forth in the fullness of time, and be of them according unto the flesh, Romans 9:5." Because the Abrahamic covenant consisted only of *historia salutis* promises, it is now ended, having been fulfilled.

[31] Günther H. Juncker, "'Children of Promise': Spiritual Paternity and Patriarch Typology in Galatians and Romans," *Bulletin for Biblical* Research 17:1 (2007): 135. Later he says: "This makes the Galatians passage with its considerably greater elaboration indispensable for a proper understanding of Rom 9:8," 149. See also Lee Irons, "Paul's Theology of Israel's Future: A Nonmillennial Interpretation of Romans 11," *Reformation and Revival* 06:2 (1997): 101–24. Note Augustine in *City of God*, IX.XV.2, on the multi-layered typology: "One portion of the earthly city became an image of the heavenly city . . . and this shadow of a city was also itself foreshadowed by another preceding figure. For Sarah's handmaid Agar, and her son, were an image of this image."

and the new."[32] Once again, Paul is expounding upon the dichotomous nature of the Abrahamic covenant.

8. The law

Central to Gordon's interpretation of Galatians is his belief that ὁ νόμος is a synecdoche for the Sinai covenant. I think this is basically true, but I also believe Gordon is unnecessarily wooden in his application of this concept. A synecdoche is a figure of speech by which a part is put for the whole. Gordon himself notes that as a figure of speech, a synecdoche has two parts: the original semantic meaning of the word (its definition) and the referential meaning (what it is figuratively being applied to). Gordon acknowledges that νόμος is the ordinary Greek term for "law," which we can define as a rule of action, a command. Paul uses the term figuratively "to *refer* to a covenant characterized by law-giving." (166, n. 4). That is, the *definition* of ὁ νόμος is not "the Sinai covenant." Yet in practice, Gordon seems to treat it as a definition rather than a figure of speech. For example, he seems unwilling to acknowledge the existence of something called "the moral law." He affirms the general concept[33] but refers to it as "compliance with our created nature," "creational realities," (184) "the duty of love," "creational imperative," (186, n. 10) and "the creational duty of *imatatio Dei*" (190, n. 21). He objects that "Westminster 19 made 'law' a universal reality, 'by which he bound him [Adam] and all his posterity to personal, entire, exact, and perpetual obedience'; whereas Paul understood ὁ νόμος to be a covenant that excluded all but the Israelites" (14). Gordon's objection is simply that the Westminster Confession used the word "law" according to its definition (WCF 19.1 even refers to it as "*a* law").[34]

---

[32] Augustine, *City of God*, IX.XV.2.

[33] "While the distinction between positive law and moral law may have been unknown to Paul, and a later development in Western philosophy, Paul evidently believed that while the Sinai legislation in its entirety disappeared with the covenant itself, some of its particular commands reflected the fundamental creational imperative to imitate (the loving) God by loving others" (186, n. 10).

[34] He makes no similar objection to the WCF using "promise" to refer to something other than the Abrahamic covenant (WCF 7.2, 5; 8.6; 14.2; 18.2; 19.1, 6) or

If "law" may only refer to the sub-eschatological Sinai covenant and its temporal life in the land of Canaan, then what becomes of the eschatological law and gospel distinction?[35] I'm afraid there will be no place to speak of the law and the gospel as two distinct ways of obtaining eternal life. What then becomes of justification by faith alone apart from works of the law? Given the way that Gordon has re-interpreted texts in Galatians that are normally understood as teaching the doctrine of penal substitutionary atonement (3:13) and justification by the law (5:4), it seems he is on a slippery slope.

9. Correcting behavior or doctrine?

There is much in Gordon's intriguing study that warrants careful consideration and even adoption (notably three Abrahamic promises, Sinai as subservient covenant of works for life in Canaan, and a distinction between the Abrahamic, Mosaic, and new covenants understood according to the *historium testamentorum*). His overall argument, however, suffers from one serious deficiency. Presumably in an effort to avoid the DP view that Paul speaks only of a misunderstanding of the Sinai covenant, rather than the Sinai covenant itself, Gordon has disregarded a crucial aspect of what Paul was arguing against. The occasion of the Jerusalem Council was that "some men came down from Judea and were teaching the brothers, 'Unless you are circumcised according to the custom of Moses, you cannot be saved'" (Acts 15:1). Gordon's only mention of this verse is a brief affirmation that the Jerusalem Council was about "correcting doctrine" (84). He says nothing at all about the specific doctrine being corrected – that people must be circumcised in order to be saved. Although he says, "Paul's issue was virtually identical to the issue addressed at the Jerusalem Council" (42) and "The problem at Galatia is nearly identical to the problem at Acts 15" (227), he holds that when Paul addresses the problem of circumcision in Galatia it has nothing

---

"faith" to refer to something other than the new covenant (WCF 3.6; 7.3, 5; 11.1–2; 14.1–3).

[35] Samuel Renihan helpfully refers to this as the *dogmatic* contrast between the law and the gospel and compares it to the contrast considered *historically* and *covenantally* as it developed in the sixteenth and seventeenth centuries. See *From Shadow to Substance*, 18–66.

to do with being saved. In fact, it has nothing to do with doctrine at all. He goes to great lengths to argue that Paul was *only* correcting behavior in Galatia. Paul's mention of justification by faith alone was merely a rhetorical lever to argue against the errant practice of Jews separating from Gentiles unless they are circumcised.

Gordon argues that "Peter was 'fearing the circumcision party,' not 'fearing God'" (87); that is, he was not withdrawing from Gentiles in order to be justified before God. He argues that the Galatians were committing the same error. Thus, it was a dispute over behavior, not doctrine. "The doctrine of justification was not disputed at Galatia" (96). What Gordon seems to neglect is a third party in Paul's letter. Paul refers to Peter acting hypocritically (thus behavior out of step with his professed belief). He also refers to the Galatians as brothers (1:11; 3:15; 4:12, 28, 31; 5:11, 13; 6:1, 18). Yet a third party is referred to as "false brothers" (2:4) "who trouble you and want to distort the gospel of Christ" (1:7; cf. 5:10). Note that these men are "preaching to you a gospel contrary to the one you received" (1:9). It is not "reading between the lines" to think that this third party is related to the false teachers of Acts 15:1. This would explain why Paul addresses the hypothetical "if righteousness comes through the law" in 2:21 — something Gordon does not seem to address. Likewise, Paul's comment in 5:4 about being justified by the law really makes little sense if justification by the law was not an issue in Galatia. Gordon argues that this refers to "a kind of 'sub-eschatological' justification" (184) for life in Canaan, which does not make sense if neither eschatological nor sub-eschatological justification was an issue for the Galatians. In sum, Gordon's claim that "there is no warrant for the common assertion that the Judaizers taught an erroneous view of justification" (86) falls flat, in my opinion.

10. The sub-eschatological law

As just noted, Gordon's insistence that "the law" refers to only the "sub-eschatological" Sinai covenant of works for temporal blessing and cursing leads him to misinterpret several key passages.[36] He paraphrases 5:4 as follows:

---

[36] Notably 3:13; 5:4.

All who wish to obey the law yourselves, and reap whatever temporal reward you may achieve thereby in the land of Canaan, go right ahead. But Christ has nothing to do with any of that—nothing to do with temporal prosperity for one nation in Canaan, and nothing to do with the obedience by which some degree thereof might be attained. (184)

He appears to be caught on the horns of an unspoken dilemma. The Sinai covenant itself is sub-eschatological. If one acknowledges that Paul is addressing eschatological inheritance through obedience to this law, then Paul must not be addressing the law itself, but rather a misunderstanding of the law (the DP reading). In order to avoid this conclusion, Gordon denies that Paul is addressing eschatological inheritance through obedience to this law.

I believe that Gordon's concerns regarding the DP "misinterpretation" reading are valid. I agree that "In Galatians (and I believe elsewhere), the problem of the law resides not in its misperception nor in its mispractice . . . The problem inheres in the covenant itself" (209).[37] However, I also believe that Paul is addressing eschatological justification through obedience to the Sinai covenant, even though that covenant itself was sub-eschatological.

The dilemma may be resolved by considering the typological nature of the Sinai covenant. Yes, the blessings and curses of Deuteronomy 28 were temporal, but they were typological of eschatological blessing and curse. Thus, as Bryan D. Estelle notes in his excellent essay on this point, by the time we get to Paul's letter

the promise of tenure in the land is over . . . Israel's disobedience has triggered the curse sanctions. Therefore, the new covenant context has essentially changed matters . . . The temporary had given way to permanence. What was prototypical has been eclipsed by what is antitypical . . . [T]he temporal life promised in the Mosaic

---

[37] Compare with John Owen on Heb. 7:12 in *An Exposition of the Epistle to the Hebrews: Hebrews 6:1–7:28*, vol. 21 of *The Works of John Owen*, ed. William H. Goold (Albany, OR: Books for the Ages, 2000), 525, where he says: "Wherefore the whole law of Moses, as given unto the Jews, whether as used or abused by them, was repugnant unto and inconsistent with the gospel . . ."

covenant portended and typified the greater "eternal life," which seems the clear position argued by the apostle Paul.[38]

Gordon recognizes a similar situation with regards to the first Abrahamic promise of numerous offspring (Gen. 15:5; 22:17; 26:4). He acknowledges it refers to Abraham's carnal offspring and that it was fulfilled prior to Christ, yet he also says that promise "appears to be glossed eschatologically by the author of Hebrews [11:12]... as does Rom. 4:17" (152, n. 78).[39]

Thus Paul really does interpret the Sinai covenant on its own terms (Lev. 18:5), but he does not limit its application to sub-eschatological life. The Sinai covenant was distinct from the broken Adamic covenant of works, yet they coincided on two points: the inheritance principle of works[40] and the moral law, allowing Paul to address issues pertaining to both, similar to how Jesus pointed the rich young ruler to Mosaic law when asked about eschatological life (Matt. 19:16–22). Importantly, Paul does not abstract the law of the Sinai covenant and make general comments about the law apart from it. He argues specifically about the Sinai covenant itself (thus many of Gordon's excellent comments regarding Paul's temporal reasoning are very helpful), but he does so with an eye towards the bigger picture the Sinai covenant typologically represented. In other words,

---

[38] Estelle, "Leviticus 18:5 and Deuteronomy 30:1–14 in Biblical Theological Development," 136–37, 118.

[39] A good case could be made that the same is true of Paul's quotation of Hab. 2:4 in Gal. 3:12. As Lightfoot *St. Paul's Epistle to the Galatians*, 138–39 notes: "In its original context the passage has reference to the temporal calamities inflicted by the Chaldean invasion. Here a spiritual meaning and general application are given to words referring primarily to special external incidents. Another portion of this same prophecy of Habakkuk (i. 5, comp. ii. 5) relating to the Chaldeans is similarly applied in a speech of St Paul, Acts xiii. 41." See also Estelle, "Leviticus 18:5 and Deuteronomy 30:1–14 in Biblical Theological Development," 135, n. 11. Israel (narrowed down to Judah) failed to keep the Mosaic law and were thus faced with destruction at the hand of Nebuchadnezzar. The Mosaic law could not save them; however, they would be spared if they believed Jeremiah's prophecy of Nebuchadnezzar's victory and surrendered themselves to him beforehand (Jer. 27:6–11).

[40] This is not to imply that the specific work required was the same in both (perfect, perpetual, personal, inward compared to outward and corporate, including ceremonial works of offering sacrifice). See n. 56 below.

"the law" may mean more than "Sinai covenant" but it does not mean less than "Sinai covenant."

11. Galatians 3:10–12

Gordon is to be commended for recognizing that Paul's quotations from the Sinai covenant in 3:10 and 3:12 are of the essence (substance) of the Sinai covenant. As mentioned previously, the common Reformed interpretation argues that Deuteronomy 27:26 and Leviticus 18:5 are not stipulations of the Sinai covenant. Rather, they are merely declarations (quotations) of another covenant—the broken Adamic covenant of works made with all mankind. A recent essay by Ben C. Dunson[41] (largely written against Gordon's prior, more abbreviated essay on Galatians[42]) takes this approach. He argues that throughout Galatians, "the law" refers "narrowly (or strictly) simply as the commandments of God . . . abstracted from the gracious covenant in which it is embedded . . ."[43] That is, "the law" means something less than the Sinai covenant. His controlling assumption is that "the Mosaic covenant (especially in prefiguring Christ's sacrifice through its own sacrificial system) is an administration of the covenant of grace, and as such, is not opposed to faith in any way whatsoever."[44] Throughout the essay Dunson presents a false

---

[41] Ben. C. Dunson, "'The Law Evidently Is Not Contrary To Faith': Galatians And The Republication Of The Covenant Of Works," *Westminster Theological Journal* 79:2 (2017), 243–66.

[42] Gordon, "Abraham and Sinai Contrasted in Galatians 3:6–14," 240–58.

[43] Dunson, "'The Law Evidently Is Not Contrary To Faith'," 262. He argues this is even the case when Paul specifically says "covenant." "The Mosaic law (note: not *covenant*) is clearly distinguished from the Abrahamic covenant in 4:21–31," 258.

[44] Dunson, "'The Law Evidently Is Not Contrary To Faith'," 266. Dunson's logic is that the Mosaic covenant was in substance the covenant of grace because it typologically revealed Christ. Note, however, that he believes the Mosaic covenant also revealed the covenant of works, yet he does not believe it is the covenant of works in substance. To be consistent, the simple fact that a covenant reveals Christ cannot be determinative of its substance. This is precisely what the subservient covenant view argued. See Owen, *An Exposition of the Epistle to the Hebrews: Hebrews 8:1-10:39*, 92–93, where he says: "If reconciliation and salvation by Christ were to be obtained not only under the old covenant, but by virtue thereof, then it must be the same for substance with the new. But this is not so; for no reconciliation with God nor

dichotomy: Paul is addressing the question of justification by works of the law, therefore he is not addressing the question of the essence of the Mosaic covenant. "Paul is writing about *individual* soteriology, not covenantal dispensations."[45] Gordon's careful attention to Paul's covenant-historical, temporal reasoning helps us recognize that Paul is in fact writing about covenantal dispensations (and how they relate to individual soteriology).

One fundamental problem with Dunson's reading of Galatians 3:12 is that it does not fit the original context of Leviticus 18:5. He claims that Paul

> recognizes this principle of justification through obedience to be taught in the law itself, although again, only when viewed simply as a set of commands not situated within the broader framework of the Mosaic covenant. Put differently, 3:12 lays out the hypothetical grounds upon which a person could be justified . . .[46]

The problem with this is twofold: Leviticus 18:5 is not a command nor a set of commands. It is the statement of a principle concerning the reward due to obedience to commands[47] and it is situated very squarely within the broader framework of the Mosaic covenant (Lev. 20:22). As Estelle has noted, later prophets call upon Leviticus 18:5 in their covenant lawsuits against Israel precisely because it was a

---

salvation could be obtained by virtue of the old covenant, or the administration of it, as our apostle disputes at large." See Renihan, *From Shadow to Substance*, 198–213.

[45] Dunson, "'The Law Evidently Is Not Contrary To Faith'," 265. After reading Dunson's essay, Gordon's insistence that Paul was dealing with wrong *behavior*, not wrong *doctrine*, makes more sense. Dunson argues that Paul is only dealing with a wrong understanding of the law. Gordon is correct to note that Paul's concern is with the practice of Gentiles being circumcised and the practice of Jewish believers segregating from Gentiles, regardless of whether the motivation is to be justified before God or not (i.e. Peter).

[46] Dunson, "'The Law Evidently Is Not Contrary To Faith'," 251.

[47] Per WCF 7.1, a reward for obedience to the law comes only by way of covenant, not by bare law. John Calvin, *Commentaries on the Epistles of Paul to the Galatians and Ephesians*, trans. William Pringle (Grand Rapids: Christian Classica Ethereal Library), Gal. 3:17, says: "Paul took into account what was certainly true, that, except by a covenant with God, no reward is due to works. Admitting, then, that the law justifies, yet before the law men could not merit salvation by works, because there was no covenant."

stipulation of the Mosaic covenant that regulated their life in the land, thus not hypothetical (Ezek. 18:9; 20:11, 13; Neh. 9:29).[48]

Dunson's position appears to be that Leviticus 18:5 was a hypothetical restatement of the Adamic covenant of works and was given only to convict Israelites of their sin, driving them to the sacrificial system where they would find forgiveness in Christ.[49] The problem is that the sacrificial system did not offer forgiveness for many violations of the laws Leviticus 18:5 refers to and the statement was not hypothetical. Those who violated the laws (including various ceremonial laws) were to be put to death.[50] As Augustine notes on Leviticus 18:5,

> Now those who were living by these works undoubtedly feared that if they did not do them, they would suffer stoning or crucifixion or something of this kind. Therefore *whoever does them*, he says, *shall live*

---

[48] Estelle, "Leviticus 18:5 and Deuteronomy 30:1-14 in Biblical Theological Development," 119–22.

[49] The OPC *Report of the Committee to Study Republication* refers to this as a declarative, administrative republication of the covenant of works (89–90).

[50] Heb. 10:28; Lev. 20; 24:14; Exod. 22:18–20; 31:14; 35:2; Num. 15:35; Deut. 13:5, 9; 17:5 (note very well 17:2, "transgresses His covenant"); 20:27; 22:21 (cf. 1 Cor. 5:13 and note well the difference). For a very good study of stoning as *cherem* punishment see Joel McDurmon, *A Consuming Fire: The Holy of Holies in Biblical Law* (Braselton, GA: Devoted Books, 2019). The sacrificial system itself operated according to Lev. 18:5, not contrary to it (Exod. 28:35; 43; 30:20–21, 30; Lev. 8:35; 10:1–2, 6, 9; 19:8; Num. 1:51; 3:10, 38; 18:3). Sin offerings were only able to be made for unintentional sins and mistakes (Lev. 4:2, 13, 22, 27) as well as for ceremonial uncleanness (Lev. 15). Paul notes that the forgiveness of sins found in Christ was not found in the old covenant sacrificial system (Acts 13:38). By Christ "everyone who believes is freed from everything from which you could not be freed by the law of Moses" (Acts 13:39). Commenting on Heb. 9:13, Owen, *An Exposition of the Epistle to the Hebrews: Hebrews 8:1–10:39*, 360, notes: "all the Levitical services and ordinances were in themselves carnal, and had carnal ends assigned unto them, and had only an obscure representation of things spiritual and eternal . . . [T]he ordinances of old, being carnal, had an efficacy unto their proper end, to purify the unclean as to the flesh . . . The rites and sacrifices of the law, by their own virtue, purified externally, and delivered only from temporary punishments." See also *The Committee to Study Republication*, 49, "By adding obedience to the ceremonial law to the essential condition of the covenant, the subservient covenant position gives Mosaic typology a fundamentally works-based character . . ."

by them, that is, shall have a reward: he will not be punished by having to undergo such a death.[51]

John Murray recognized that it was not possible to interpret Leviticus 18:5 as a hypothetical restatement of the covenant of works precisely because of its covenantal context.

[Lev. 18:5] does not appear in a context that deals with legal righteousness as opposed to that of faith. Lev. 18:5 is in a context in which the claims of God upon his redeemed and covenant people are being asserted and urged upon Israel... [It] refers not to the life accruing from doing in a legalistic framework but to the blessing attendant upon obedience in a redemptive and covenant relationship to God.[52]

This is precisely why he rejected the doctrine of the Adamic covenant *of works*.

In connection with the promise of life it does not appear justifiable to appeal, as frequently has been done, to the principle enunciated in certain texts (cf. Lev. 18:5; Rom. 10:5; Gal. 3:12), 'This do and thou shalt live'. The principle asserted in these texts is the principle of equity, that righteousness is always followed by the corresponding award.[53]

---

[51] Augustine, *Augustine's Commentary on Galatians*, ed. Eric Plumer (Oxford: Oxford University Press, 2003), 159. Noteworthy for the question of sub-eschatological righteousness and temporal reward through obedience to the Sinai covenant, Augustine continues, "But nevertheless, as I have said, there really is a kind of earthly and carnal righteousness (so to speak), for even the Apostle himself calls it righteousness when he says in another passage: *according to the righteousness that is by the law, I was blameless* (Phil. 3:6)."

[52] John Murray, *The Epistle to the Romans*, 2 vol. (1959; reprint, Grand Rapids: William B. Eerdmans Publishing Company, 1997), II:249.

[53] John Murray, "The Adamic Administration," in *Collected Writings*, vol. II (Edinburgh; Carlisle, PA: Banner of Truth Trust, 1977), 55. He continues: "From the promise of the Adamic administration we must dissociate all notions of meritorious reward. The promise of confirmed integrity and blessedness was one annexed to an obedience that Adam owed and, therefore, was a promise of grace. All that Adam could have claimed on the basis of equity was justification and life as long as he perfectly obeyed, but not confirmation so as to insure indefectibility. Adam could

As chairman of the OPC Committee on Texts and Proof Texts from 1940-51, Murray added Leviticus 18:5 (and Matt. 19:17) as a proof text to WCF 19.6. "The promises of it [the law], in like manner, show them [believers] God's approbation of obedience, and what blessings they may expect upon the performance thereof . . ."[54]

Any attempt to understand Leviticus 18:5 and Paul's quotation of it as an abstraction from the Sinai covenant (rather than a stipulation of the covenant itself) fails exegetically. Placing Leviticus 18:5 in the context of a Mosaic covenant of grace undermines the Adamic covenant of works and thus the eschatological law and gospel distinction.[55] Recognizing Leviticus 18:5 as a summary statement of a typological Sinai covenant of works for life in the land of Canaan[56] fits

---

claim the fulfilment of the promise if he stood the probation, but only on the basis of God's faithfulness, not on the basis of justice" (56).

[54] *The Westminster Confession of Faith and Catechisms as adopted by The Orthodox Presbyterian Church* (Willow Grove, PA: The Committee on Christian Education of the Orthodox Presbyterian Church, 2005), viii-x, 91. The original Westminster Standards did not reference Lev. 18:5 anywhere. It did cite Gal. 3:10, 12 and Rom. 10:5 in 7.2, which Murray said was unjustified.

[55] Guy Waters recognizes Murray's point regarding the redemptive context of Lev. 18:5, even going so far as to quote him on it. Yet he argues specifically for the confessional covenant of works from Rom. 10:5. He is not entirely clear how that is possible. He argues that the moral law itself continues to express "the connection between 'obedience' and 'life' expressed by the moral law in the covenant of works," even when the moral law is given as a rule of life in the Mosaic covenant of grace. The problem is that Lev. 18:5 is not a command (moral law). It is a principle regarding how the moral law functions ("the connection between 'obedience' and 'life'"). As such, it must be a principle that is equally true in the covenant of works and the covenant of grace, including the new covenant (which led Murray to reject the principle of the covenant of works and add Lev. 18:5 to WCF 19.6). Waters cannot maintain that Lev. 18:5 expresses the connection between obedience and life found in the covenant of works and that it also "refer[s] to the sanctificational works of a redeemed person within the covenant community . . ." See Guy Waters, "The Mosaic Covenant and the Covenant of Works: An Analysis of Romans 10:5," in *The Law is Not of Faith*, 210-39.

[56] It is important to understand that the Sinai covenant operated upon the same *principle* as the Adamic covenant of works, but not the exact same *conditions*. The Adamic covenant required personal, entire, exact, and perpetual obedience while the Sinai covenant enforced outward and corporate obedience to the letter and allowed sub-eschatological atonement for various ceremonial sins. Abraham Booth, *An Essay on the Kingdom of Christ* (Sacramento, CA: Reformed Libertarian, 2015), loc. 440, 1090, says: "Jehova acknowledged all those for *his* people, and himself as *their* God, who

the original context, makes sense of Paul's citation, and upholds the law and gospel distinction necessary for the doctrine of justification by faith alone.

---

performed an external obedience to his commands, even though in their hearts disaffected to him . . . Health and long life, riches, honours, and victory over their enemies, were promised by Jehovah to their external obedience. (Ex 25:25,26; 28:25–28; Lev 26:3–14; Deut 7:12–24; 8:7–9; 11:13–17; 28:3–13)." See John Erskine, "I. The Nature of the Sinai Covenant," *Theological Dissertations* (London: Dilly, 1765), 5, 47, where he says: "[God] appeared chiefly as a temporal prince, and therefore gave laws intended rather to direct the outward conduct, than to regulate the actings of the heart . . . obedience to the letter of the law, even when it did not flow from a principle of faith and love . . . He who yielded an external obedience to the law of Moses, was termed righteous, and had a claim in virtue of this his obedience to the land of Canaan, so that doing these things he lived by them (Lev. 18:5; Deut. 5:33). Hence, says Moses (Deut. 6:25)[.]" See also A. W. Pink, *The Divine Covenants* (Prisbrary Publishing, 2012), loc. 2415. And see Thomas Scott, *The Holy Bible, with Explanatory Notes, Practical Observations, and Copious Marginal References,* 6 vols. 5th ed. (London: Baldwin, 1822), 205, "The covenant which God made with Israel at Sinai required outward obedience to the letter of the law. . . The outward covenant was made with the nation, entitling them to outward advantages, upon the condition of outward national obedience." Thus, Dunson's objection that God could not make another covenant of works with fallen sinners is misplaced. Under the Noahic covenant, God gives fallen, unrepentant sinners outside of Christ rain and sun (Matt. 5:45). There is no principled reason why God could not suspend those same blessings (or even more superlative temporal blessings) upon condition of obedience to the Sinai law. See John Erskine, "I. The Nature of the Sinai Covenant," 15–16. Dunson quotes John Owen to explain how the Mosaic covenant declared the original Adamic covenant of works without re-making it with Israel. This is correct. But Owen also held to the subservient covenant view. See Owen, *An Exposition of the Epistle to the Hebrews: Hebrews 8:1-10:39,* 83, 101, "The covenant of works had its promises, but they were all remunerative, respecting an antecedent obedience in us; (so were all those which were peculiar unto the covenant of Sinai) . . . [H]e moreover prescribed unto them laws, rules, and terms of obedience, whereon they should hold and enjoy that land, with all the privileges annexed unto the possession thereof." Finally, God's longsuffering mercy in withholding the full curse of the Sinai covenant from Israel was rooted in the Abrahamic promise to give them the land (Gen. 15:10-11; Exod. 32:14; Num. 14:20; Deut. 28:26; Jer. 7:33; Psalm 106:8, 23, 44–45). Once that was fulfilled completely under Solomon (1 Kings 4:20-25; 8:56), Israel was split in two and the 10 tribes were annihilated according to the Sinai curse. God remained longsuffering towards Judah until the promised seed of Abraham (which had been narrowed to David) was born. Once that happened, Judah was destroyed in AD 70 as the full curse of Sinai was unleashed upon them.

12. Galatians 2:19

I believe Gordon is probably correct that "through the law" in 2:19 refers to "the law's own teaching about its temporary character" (102), which Lightfoot refers to as the "economical purpose" of the law.[57] Though I think it could possibly refer to the pedagogical use of the law.

13. Galatians 3:13

I disagree with Gordon's claim that 3:13 does not refer to the Gentiles' redemption in Christ, nor to the Jews' eternal redemption in Christ, but rather to the Jews' redemption from the temporal curse of Sinai through its abrogation. I don't think his interpretation is possible. Per above, I believe this is best understood as Paul reasoning from the typological Sinai covenant curses to the eschatological curse Christ bore in our place (penal substitutionary atonement).

14. Galatians 3:19, 23

I believe that Gordon is correct to point out that whatever purpose of the law Paul refers to here, it served that purpose only until the new covenant ("faith" refers to the new covenant in the *historia salutis*, not the existential experience of faith in the *ordo salutis*). Thus, his argument that the verses refer to the preservation of the Abrahamic lineage is compelling. The law served the role of a protective guardian until the Jews came of age, which fits well with 4:2.

15. Galatians 3:26–27

I think Gordon is mistaken to read this as a comparison between old and new ceremonies (circumcision and baptism[58]). I suggest the

---

[57] Lightfoot, *St. Paul's Epistle to the Galatians*, 118.

[58] The ritual of baptism may not even be the immediate reference here. I believe Fred Karlson is correct that it would be much better to *translate* ἐβαπτίσθητε (as "placed into, plunging, united to, or washed") rather than simply transliterating it as "baptized" throughout the NT. He offers a possible translation of v. 27 as "For as many of you as have been *placed* into Christ have put on Christ." Thus it would refer

distinction between Jew and Greek, male and female, slave and free refers not to how they related to circumcision, but how they related to inheritance. As Gordon notes, chapter 4 continues and focuses the question of "Who will inherit the third reality pledged to Abraham and Sarah?" (167). Free, Jewish males inherited the land of Canaan, while slaves, Greeks, and females did not (Num. 36). These distinctions do not apply to the eschatological inheritance of the new covenant.

Conclusion

Promise, Law, Faith helpfully challenges the dominant Reformed reading of Galatians by insisting we must understand Paul's temporal reasoning and his covenant distinctions. The belief that the Abrahamic, Mosaic, and new covenant are all, in substance, the same covenant does not match Paul's thought in his letter to the Galatians. "[W]e may say with entire confidence that 'these are two covenants' (Gal. 4:24) can never be responsibly construed as 'these are one covenant'" (208).[59] Gordon's recognition that Paul's citation of Leviticus 18:5 describes the Sinai covenant of works itself, rather than a misunderstanding or abuse of it, is a crucial foundation for the eschatological law and gospel distinction, even though Gordon himself hinders this foundation by too rigidly limiting Paul's analysis of the Sinai covenant to temporal blessing and curse. Gordon's division of the Abrahamic covenant into three distinct promises made concerning different seed (carnal, national, corporate seed and singular, Messianic seed) is very helpful in making sense of Paul's

---

to identification or union with Christ (rather than to the ritual which symbolizes that union). Fred Karlson, "What is the Primary Meaning of Baptism? Some Translational Difficulties," in *Northwest ETS Meeting, March 4, 2006*, notes: "The ceremony of water baptism surely signifies, among other things, the putting on of the garments of Christ's righteousness. However, it introduces a theological difficulty if one equates the two [ceremony and union] by explicitly mentioning 'water' in Galatians 3:27." This can be found at https://bible.org/article/what-primary-meaning-baptism-some-translational-difficulties. Accessed 2 October 20.

[59] As previously noted, Dunson does precisely that. In Dunson, "'The Law Evidently Is Not Contrary To Faith'," 258, he says: "The Mosaic law (note: not *covenant*) is clearly distinguished from the Abrahamic covenant in 4:21–31."

argumentation in Galatians (even if Gordon himself does not draw out all of the necessary implications of this).

Gordon's denial that justification by faith alone was challenged by the Judaizers, combined with his insistence on the sub-eschatological nature of Paul's view of the Sinai covenant, however, leads him to misinterpret key passages that are foundational to the doctrine of justification by faith alone as well as penal substitutionary atonement. His doctrine of the moral law is also unnecessarily impaired by *defining* ὁ νόμος as the Sinai covenant. While I sympathize with Gordon's goals, I think more care must be taken in balancing biblical and systematic theology.[60] In my opinion, the covenant theology of the seventeenth-century particular Baptists[61] struck the right balance between biblical theology (including the *historia testamentorum* — compare WCF 7.5–6 which conflates the biblical covenants as one in substance with 2LBC 7.3) and systematic theology. However, much of that work has been polemical in nature, arguing against paedobaptism. The church would be greatly benefited from more work applying the Particular Baptist understanding of covenant theology to biblical studies. I am thankful for Gordon nudging us in that direction.

---

[60] In a related manner, Gordon's zealousness for his position seems to lead him to carelessly overstate the deficiencies of those he disagrees with, such as his insistence that DP is "reading between the lines" while he is just "reading the lines," and his well-known comparison of John Murray to a drunk uncle who never wrote on Galatians because he couldn't make sense of it (Gordon, "Abraham and Sinai Contrasted in Galatians 3:6–14," 251 and "Reflections on Auburn Theology," 118).

[61] This view was not limited to the seventeenth century but continued into the early twentieth century. The view was obscured for a short time but has been rediscovered in recent years. It has come to be referred to popularly as "1689 Federalism." See Renihan, *From Shadow to Substance*; Pascal Denault, *The Distinctiveness of Baptist Covenant Theology* (Birmingham, AL: Solid Ground Christian Books, 2013); and *Covenant Theology: From Adam to Christ*. The view is an elaboration upon the subservient covenant view, recognizing the new covenant alone as the covenant of grace (union with Christ) and all other post-fall covenants as distinct from but subservient to the new.

Book Reviews

Canon, Covenant and Christology:
Rethinking Jesus and the Scriptures of Israel,
New Studies in Biblical Theology
Matthew Barrett
(InterVarsity Press, 2020, 387pp.),
reviewed by Craig A. Carter[*]

The essential thesis of this book is that it is impossible to take seriously Jesus' claims that he fulfills the Hebrew Scriptures unless one supposes that he consciously and with full comprehension of the implications believed the Scriptures to be the inspired, inerrant, and authoritative word of God.

If this is true, and if Jesus is Lord, then a high view of biblical inspiration and authority rests not on a few proof texts from the pastoral epistles but on the NT witness as a whole. It also means that acknowledging the Lordship of Christ logically entails having a high view of Scripture. The two are so intertwined that all attempts to separate them apart ultimately fail. It cannot be said that Jesus and the early church "adopted" the Hebrew Scriptures because that presumes that a time existed when Jesus and the early church existed and then decided to adopt the Hebrew Scriptures. There was no such time; it is more accurate to say that "the Scriptures give birth to Jesus himself and are the genesis of his church" (197). From the perspective of faith, the Hebrew Scriptures (i.e., OT) are basic to everything. Barrett says, "It was not a matter of reading Jesus back into the Old Testament: the Old Testament itself was the seed that blossomed into its own fulfillment with the coming of the messianic king" (201). The unity of the Bible, therefore, is rooted in the fit between what was promised and predicted in the OT and the fulfillment of those promises and predictions in the NT.

---

[*] Craig A. Carter, is Professor of Theology, Tyndale University and author of *Contemplating God with the Great Tradition: Recovering Trinitarian Classical Theism* (Baker Academic, 2021).

Barrett also argues that the emergence of the church out of Judaism occurred because of a disagreement over Jesus' messianic identity:

> The great divide between Jews who rejected Jesus and Jews who followed him comes down to this: the former did not believe Jesus was the fulfillment of the scriptures of Israel, but the latter did and based everything on that foundational belief. (200)

This perspective is crucial because it undermines the "Jewish versus Christian" frame that is the basis for anti-Semitism. It shows that belief in Jesus divided Jews from one another and Gentiles joined the debate on both sides. Faith in Jesus as Messiah is more basic than one's Jewish or Gentile ethnicity. Christian believers are more fundamentally united with believing Jews than with unbelieving Gentiles.

The Jewish leaders thought they had proven that Jesus was not the Messiah by having him crucified. If he was the Messiah, they thought, that could never have happened. But the resurrection of Jesus from the dead demonstrated how wrong they were, and this is why the NT sees the proclamation of the risen Lord Jesus Christ to the whole world as the central task of the church. In the resurrection, God makes it plain that Jesus is, in fact, the Messianic King and the divine Son of God. This is good news because if the king has come then the kingdom has come with him. To bow to him is to be in the kingdom of God.

The book consists of seven chapters. In the first chapter, Barrett discusses the nature of biblical theology and argues that the key to understanding how the Hebrew Scriptures point to Christ is to have a strong understanding of divine authorial intent as the key to hermeneutics. We need to see the OT as a unified narrative with the Messiah at the center. Christ is the real subject of the OT and God is the speaker.

In chapter 2, Barrett highlights the covenantal nature of the OT. The prophets are the prosecutors of the covenant treaty on behalf of Yahweh. Here we can see that the message of the Hebrew Scriptures cannot be reconciled with the nineteenth-century higher critical inversion by which Wellhausen and his followers claimed that the prophets were the real founders of Israel's religion and that the Pentateuch was an exilic creation. This revisionist approach renders the Bible's own narrative false. Barrett stresses:

> Given the Pentateuch's foundational role to all revelation that followed there is no question that Israel believed the Torah originated from Yahweh himself, nor did Israel doubt the Torah to be authoritative and sufficient to instruct her in the way of the covenant. (63)

Jesus, says Barrett, assumes that the OT has a "canon consciousness" and that the canon was focussed on him. Therefore, Barrett says, "Jesus is the canon" (93). This is what Luke 24 teaches.

In chapters 3 and 4, Barrett looks at Matthew and John as case studies in how the NT proclaims that "Jesus is the fulfillment of the Law and the Prophets" (97). He stresses the entire structure of the narrative of Jesus' life and works as presented in the Gospels, as opposed to focussing only on specific, individual prophecies. Many modern readers miss the intertextual echoes and allusions to OT passages, types, stories and images, because of a lack of familiarity with the contents of the OT and a shallow comprehension of the intention of the Gospel writers. Barrett spells out these fundamental points for good reading of the NT in detail.

In chapter 5, Barrett examines Christ's covenantal obedience as his means of fulfilling the redemptive promises and types of the OT. Whereas Israel persistently disobeyed the terms of the covenant and failed to keep the law, Jesus perfectly obeyed the law and kept the covenant as the New Israel. The mission of the incarnate Son involves fulfilling all righteousness and thus attaining redemption for God's covenant people. Barrett emphasizes that the nature of this obedience is actually obedience to the Scriptures as the Word of God (204). According to Barrett, an important part of the disagreement between Jesus and the Pharisees was Jesus' rejection of the "tradition of the elders" as being on a par with the authority of the written Scriptures. The point is that Jesus had a very high view of the authority of Scripture (232). Yet, Jesus also held up his own teaching as authoritative in a way that angered his opponents.

Chapter 6 moves from description of what Jesus did in his incarnation to the question of who Jesus must be in order for him legitimately to do what he did. If he is the one predicted by the Scriptures and the fulfillment of the redemptive plan of God revealed in the Scriptures, what is his ontological status? By what authority does Jesus claim to be the one of whom the Scriptures speak? (247).

It is at this point that Barrett's book models theological method for us today. What we must do is to "look to the mission of the Son to discover the attitude of the Son toward the Scriptures" (204). What Barrett is doing here is reasoning from the economic activity of the Son back toward the ontology that such activity presupposes. This is how the church historically has done theology. In the twentieth century, however, the focus on the economic Trinity tended to crowd out all talk of the ontological Trinity and this tendency toward historicism had implications for all of theology, not just the foundational doctrine of the Trinity. Barrett's work is like a case study illustrating this fact—a case study in the authority of Scripture.

Barrett's argument cannot be dismissed as a matter of systematic theologians reading dogma into the text. This is so, in part, because of the extensive exegetical work he has done in order to demonstrate that the unity of Scripture around Christ as its central theme is found throughout the canon. He sums it up by saying, "If Christ interpreted the old Scriptures 'with authority,' as if he were their author, it was because, in the final ontological analysis, that is what he is" (249). Christology flows out of the biblical themes of promise and fulfillment. Barrett shows that the status of Jesus as the Son of the Father in the Gospel of John indicates a relationship best termed "eternal generation" in which the Son is equal ontologically to the Father and is so eternally (260). As Barrett puts it, "Such ontological unity defines the eternal Trinity but was revealed in history when the Son's supernatural works were performed" (274). Barrett strives to show how the incarnation, as the work of God in history, is meant to point us back to the eternal being of the triune God who exists prior to the incarnation and who exists eternally. The Son "reveals" the Father (278) and in so doing reveals the triune nature of Israel's God.

Chapter 7 extends the argument of the book in such a way as to explicate the dogmatic implications of the kind of biblical theology done in chapters 1–6. Here Barrett discusses the Evangelical doctrine of biblical inerrancy and claims that we need to develop a more theological case for inerrancy than has been done thus far. Like Barth, we need a doctrine of biblical authority that is based on Christology, but unlike Barth, we need to clarify that calling the Bible inerrant is not undermining the freedom of God. Barth resisted the doctrine of inerrancy because he felt it enslaved the Word of God to words on a page—a "dead letter" (312). Barrett argues that this critique ignores "the covenantal framework of history that God himself has structured and revealed" (313), which Barret has described at length in this book. Barrett could have strengthened his argument here by showing that Barth's objection also can be answered by a more robust doctrine of divine providence in which divine authorship is not imperiled in the slightest by human beings acting within the economy of grace producing texts exactly as God desires. As it is, however, Barrett rightly accuses Barth's view of Scripture as not being Christological enough (315). Barth needs to put *more* stock in divine authorial intent, and the way to do that is to see the divine unity of Scripture by reading it Christologically. Barrett's conclusion is that the Evangelical doctrine of inerrancy "has a Christological foundation that is far sturdier than that of its critics" (315).

This book is a major contribution to the renewal of theology in our day because it breaks down the barriers erected by modernist biblical criticism between exegesis and dogmatics. In so doing, it points the way forward to the way to do theology using a classical, premodern method that does not suffer from the silo effect of dividing exegetical and biblical theology from dogmatic theology. In the case of the doctrine of biblical inspiration, we clearly need to formulate our doctrine in dogmatic terms but on the basis of exegetical conclusions derived from a biblical-theological interpretation of the canon as a whole.

The Fulfillment of the Promises of God:
An Explanation of Covenant Theology,
Richard P. Belcher, Jr.
(Ross-shire, UK: Christian Focus Publications, 2020, 281pp.),
reviewed by Samuel Renihan

Dr. Richard P. Belcher, Jr. currently serves as the John D. and Frances M. Gwin Professor of Old Testament, and is the Academic Dean at Reformed Theological Seminary in Charlotte, NC. His book *The Fulfillment of the Promises of God* is, as its subtitle states, an explanation of covenant theology. After an introduction, the book works its way through the covenants, chronologically, from Adam to Noah, to Abraham, to Moses, to David, to Christ. This exposition of the covenants is followed by chapters evaluating variations in covenantal thought within the modern Presbyterian tradition, such as those of O. Palmer Robertson, John Murray, and Meredith Kline, concluding with chapters interacting with Reformed Baptists and Progressive Covenantalism.

In the Introduction, Belcher states that "The aim of this book will be to set forth standard Reformed covenant theology as exemplified in the Scriptures and explained in the WCF [Westminster Confession of Faith]" (21). If one is familiar with "standard Reformed covenant theology" then the contents of the book will be unsurprising. Belcher advances the argument that God made a covenant of works with Adam, which he broke. After this, God revealed the covenant of grace, and the Abrahamic, Mosaic, and Davidic covenants constitute its pre-incarnation administration, while the new covenant constitutes the post-incarnation administration of the same singular covenant of grace. This covenant of grace is the historical outworking of the covenant of redemption.

I found the style of the book to be very beneficial. It is written in a charitable, friendly, and encouraging manner. In a subject prone to debates and divides, Belcher's style is one to be noted, commended, and emulated. One gets the impression that one could disagree with Belcher and yet speak openly with him about what he has proposed. Ministers are not to be quarrelsome (2 Tim. 2:24), and Belcher's literature sets an example for all other ministers and ministerial candidates.

Belcher's friendliness is evidenced strongly in his inclusion of sections interacting with variations of covenant theology within the Presbyterian tradition, and sections explaining and briefly interacting with Baptist covenantal traditions. In these latter sections, Belcher has clearly given serious attention to the Baptist literature with which he interacts, and he shows a sincere desire to commend the good he finds in them. This brotherly dialogue is sorely lacking in many spheres.

As Belcher has charitably interacted with alternate models, within and without his tradition, so I desire to offer constructive criticisms to what Belcher has proposed in his book, focusing on a desire for a greater discussion of foundational methodology and terminology. The scope of the subject is large, and the book would have swollen considerably, but in my opinion, such a section is an absolute necessity for this subject and for a book attempting to offer a comprehensive consideration of it.

To be specific, three things stand out. The first is the issue of federal headship. Belcher asserts in a brief discussion of the definition of a covenant that "descendants are included" in covenants (18). Later, he states that "This is the normal way that covenants operate" (73) and that "Whenever a covenant is made, future descendants are included in the covenant" (86). Elsewhere, Belcher asserts that covenants operate on the basis of "a representative principle" (26). These two assertions are not opposed to one another, but they are not equal. It is faithful to the Scriptures to say that covenants operate on the basis of representation or federal headship, but then we must state that whomever the federal head represents are those who are included. This may, or may not be, one's natural descendants. Covenantal membership is not determined by a default inclusion of descendants, but by God's designation of whom the federal head represents.

The distinction is important because the failure to make it affects Belcher's view of who is the federal head of the Abrahamic covenant. Abraham, Belcher states, is merely head of the covenant in the sense that "he received the promise of its continuance in the line of his natural and spiritual descendants" (70, n. 28). Preceding this is Belcher's commitment to the idea that the Abrahamic covenant is the covenant of grace. Because Christ is head of that covenant, Abraham cannot be head of the Abrahamic covenant. Under this system, Abraham is an especially privileged believer whose descendants are included by default, but he is not the covenant-head of the Abrahamic people, Christ is.

But I question, what if God covenanted with Abraham, on behalf of his descendants, to give them blessed life in Canaan and to bring forth the blessing for the nations (Christ) from one of their descendants? And what if all those who descend from Abraham, or who become his descendants through circumcision, have a right and title to this promise by virtue of Abraham's headship? That is, what if the Abrahamic covenant, the covenant of circumcision, is distinct from the covenant of grace, and yet subservient to it? It seems that, for some, Paul's arguments against Judaizing errors in the NT, proving that the Christ for all the nations was always God's plan by pointing to Christ in God's dealings with Abraham, has been taken too far to equate the Abrahamic covenant and the covenant of grace.

The second item of methodology and terminology which deserves greater attention is an uncritical use of the terminology of "administration." For example, even in a section entitled "The Historical Administration of the Covenant" (45–46) there is no definition offered for what it means to "administer" a covenant or what an "administration" is. Belcher is working within the WCF tradition and appropriating its common language, so it could be argued that the definitions are assumed. Context reveals that Belcher is discussing the outward, visible, practical elements of the covenant, but the term "administration" needs sharper definition.

This becomes clearer in the third item which demands deeper discussion—typology. Typology is not defined, but often used, in this book. Types are treated as analogous to their antitypes, but the question of whether they are the same thing as their antitypes, though in a lesser form, is not answered or specified.

When contrasting the Mosaic covenant and the new covenant, Belcher states that "The covenant under Moses partook of the provisional, shadowy nature of types and ordinances . . . that all foreshadowed Christ to come" (133). The reader is left to infer what this means. Belcher gives some indication when he states that these were "sufficient and efficacious" but "could not perfect those who drew near" (133–34). The question one must then ask is, if the ordinances of the Mosaic covenant could not, in themselves, perfect those who drew near to God through them, then are they the same thing as their antitypes? And if they are not the same, that is, if animal sacrifices are not Christ's sacrifice, then how do we reconcile the relationship of the pre-incarnation "administration" of the covenant to the covenant of grace itself? The covenant of grace's ordinances did not and could not, in themselves, provide saving grace?

As a Baptist, this is perhaps the single strongest point I would wish to emphasize. An indiscriminate use of "administration" in an undefined context of typology generates a mist within which "standard" Reformed covenant theology can perpetuate itself despite significant internal and exegetical strain.

For example, Belcher notes that "The sanctions of the Mosaic covenant focus on temporal and material blessings and curses" (94) and that "Israel loses the land because she breaks the covenant and lives in disobedience to God" (90). But on the other hand, Belcher states that "There is a works principle still operative in the Covenant of Grace in a secondary sense related to the second use of the law" (92–93). Belcher means that the law reminds Israelites of their inability to keep the covenant of works, thus pointing them to Christ. All of this, a works-principle for life in the land, and an unkeepable works-principle echoing Eden and pointing to Christ, Belcher argues, is "part-and-parcel of the Covenant of Grace" (88). There are considerable internal tensions in this presentation of the nature of the Mosaic covenant's ordinances and the purposes of the law.

As historical theology demonstrates, many Presbyterians and Baptists will find this unsatisfactory. It may perpetuate the WCF model, but it seems more a case of a system driving exegesis than exegesis building a system. In my view, Belcher's commendable attention to the text makes his systematic conclusions perplexing. He is trapped by his own tradition. The WCF may be considered a "standard," but the truth is that it represents only one particular view of covenant theology from within the diversity of Reformed covenant theology in its own day.

Whether Baptist or Presbyterian, there is a rich, related covenantal heritage in the tradition of John Cameron, the Congregationalists (Bolton, Burroughs, Goodwin, Owen), and the Particular Baptists who understood the Mosaic covenant to be neither the covenant of works, nor the covenant of grace, but a national covenant of works, subservient to the covenant of grace. This model resolves many of the tensions Belcher creates in his own treatment, but the WCF disallows it.

In conclusion, Belcher's book is friendly, positive, and responsible. It promotes conversation and camaraderie, not caricatures and curt dismissals. It accomplishes its stated goal. However, until Belcher and other dear Presbyterian brethren are able to work in covenant theology beyond the boundaries of WCF and the mists of "administration," I fear that they will neither settle internal debates nor convince sincere other-minded brethren in the Lord. Despite these disagreements, we agree on much. And in Belcher's own words, "Agreement on these major theological questions is significant and is something Baptists and Presbyterians can be thankful for" (231).

Politics after Christendom:
Political Theology in a Fractured World,
David VanDrunen
(Grand Rapids: Zondervan Academic, 2020, 400pp.),
reviewed by Micah Renihan

Over the last decade, David VanDrunen has been writing books exploring the topics of two kingdoms theology and natural law. Each book stands on its own, and yet the books clearly build on each other as well. The first two works were both published in 2010. One was a more popular level treatment of two kingdoms theology, *Living in God's Two Kingdoms*. The other was a historical study entitled *Natural Law and the Two Kingdoms: A Study in the Development of Reformed Social Thought*. In 2014 VanDrunen released *Divine Covenants and Moral Order: A Biblical Theology of Natural Law*. Following in this sequence comes the latest work (2020), *Politics after Christendom: Political Theology in a Fractured World*. Those who have read the previous works will find much that is familiar in this latest piece, along with a significant amount of new material as VanDrunen more directly explores the field of politics from the perspectives of two kingdoms theology and (especially) natural law.

The book is divided into two parts. The first part (chs. 1–6) lays out the theology that VanDrunen is exploring while the second part (chs. 7–12) discusses several particular areas of concern or difficulty. The theology of part 1 is largely a revisiting of material found in VanDrunen's previous works, especially *Divine Covenants and Moral Order*. Here he gives more substance to various claims that were made in those books while providing summaries of claims that were previously given greater space. Chapter 1 is particularly helpful in directing the course of the remainder of the book since it lays out some of the basic principles that drive the theology he develops. VanDrunen argues that a Christian political theology will see government as legitimate but provisional and common (not redemptive) but accountable (to God). Charitable readers will find that these pages assuage many of the fears and criticisms that are often carelessly directed at the two kingdoms theology VanDrunen has worked hard to defend. Chapters 2–4 work through the biblical data that form the backbone for VanDrunen's conclusions with a special emphasis on the way that the Noahic covenant forms the basis for common grace relationships and government. Chapter 5 picks up on some important themes from *Divine Covenants and Moral Order*, particularly the connection between natural law and wisdom. VanDrunen argues that wisdom is the observation of patterns in the world which then inform how we ought to act in concrete situations (140). Natural law, he argues, is grasped as we mature in the pursuit of wisdom. This pursuit of wisdom and natural law is essential in understanding how a political theory should be developed. The final chapter of part 1 provides a sketch for how Christians ought to engage in public life. He reminds us that we are sojourners and exiles who do not find their permanent home here and yet are called to participate in the life of the community in which we are now placed. Abraham, Israel during exile, and the NT epistles are used to describe what it looks like to live as sojourners and pilgrims with reference to this world. We are to seek a "just commonality" (159) and to seek this with an attitude that "recognizes the fleetingness of life" (166), has "confidence in the Lord" (167), and is "charitable, compassionate, and cheerful" (168).

Each chapter in part 2 takes on two related topics and explores them together. Chapter 7 discusses pluralism and religious liberty. VanDrunen argues that a "common" political entity needs to be open to people of every religious persuasion since the Noahic covenant is not meant to be redemptive. The best way to achieve this pluralism is through a limited government that leaves individuals free to follow their conscience on many potentially challenging moral and ideological issues. Chapter 8, on family and commerce, first argues for a conception of the family that is derived from natural law. VanDrunen concludes that this conception is a family that is "monogamous, heterosexual, and permanent" (221). In the second half of the chapter he argues for the proper place of commerce. Commerce is good and to be pursued, but not to be made into an idol. Without being overly specific on what form commerce ought to take, he argues for a market economy over a command economy.

Chapters 9–12 build on each other quite heavily. VanDrunen develops a hierarchy in which justice is the foundation of laws which are the foundation of government (250). It is critical for his argument that this hierarchy be noted and maintained. Throughout these chapters VanDrunen works to provide what is often a middle way between competing views on these issues. He argues that the Noahic covenant points to a conception of justice that has elements of many modern and traditional conceptions of justice without being an exact fit for any of them. He builds on the principle of the *lex talionis* as a starting point for many of his discussions and combines that with the previous arguments for a limited government and a pluralistic society. He concludes that justice, as it is worked out in social settings, will preserve negative rights (things that others may not do to you such as killing you) but will usually not apply to positive or welfare rights. Chapter 10 introduces a pivotal argument for this book: that laws are polycentric not monocentric. Law develops from custom as humans interact with one another and it is expressed and enforced in multiple ways (polycentric) rather than just from the government (monocentric). This becomes key for the remainder of the book. If the source of law is polycentric then the government does not have the sole claim to law and its enforcement (VanDrunen regularly points to third party mediation and personal security details as examples of enforcement of laws outside of the government). Because law precedes government, the polycentric nature of law gives VanDrunen the resources needed to describe what forms of resistance to the government are legitimate and what level of authority the government has. He acknowledges that a society may give to the government a greater level of authority than what it would naturally have, but, even then, if the customs of the people (where law originates) do not match a law a government has made there is a *de facto* nullification of that law.

The final chapter is an interesting evaluation of the liberal and conservative traditions of political thought. In this chapter the terms "liberal" and "conservative" are not used in the same sense they are popularly used today (where liberal = democrat and conservative = republican) but in their traditional understanding. VanDrunen attempts to identify the "one big idea" of each group. For liberals it is "the peaceful coexistence of individuals and institutions that hold different conceptions of ultimate truth and seek their own distinctive ends, achieved through voluntary cooperation and protection of basic rights" (365). For conservatives it is the emphasis on "long-acquired and hard-won wisdom" (369). He argues these ideas are not entirely antithetical to each other and may be paired together to form a conservative liberalism which matches the political teachings of the Noahic covenant. With this conservative liberalism, VanDrunen is able to briefly turn to a critique of the two common political traditions in America today, which he identifies as progressivism (associated with the political left) and nationalism (associated with the political right). Both groups come under criticisms for the ways they have departed from a natural law and Noahic covenant conception of government.

One of the important features of this book is the way the chapters build on each other. The theology of part 1 is essential to understanding the way the topics of part 2 are addressed. Even within each part there is a progression from one chapter to the next that needs to be followed. Readers must resist the urge to read the final chapters of the book without first working through the earlier material.

VanDrunen writes from his own religious and theological tradition: Reformed theology. However, he writes in such a way that the book should have broad appeal among Evangelicals of various stripes. He interacts with authors from many and various traditions and points of view along the way. The tone of the book is irenic, not combative; he strives to be fair with all those with which he interacts. There are several concepts in this book that are not common among the usual *loci* of theology (since politics is not one of the major *loci* of theology). For those who are new to political theory, VanDrunen does an able job of explaining the concepts in direct ways before he begins to interact with them. His handling of Scripture is excellent. Often times it seems that he draws conclusions in tentative ways when he has provided enough support to make those conclusions more definitively.

Being a neophyte in regard to political theory, I hesitate to offer too much in the way of critique of such a fine book. However, there were some questions still in my mind. For one thing, this book must walk a difficult line and it struggles to do so. On the one hand, it is a work of theology, and VanDrunen wants to show how his views comport with theology. On the other hand, it is often more of a work of *natural* theology, and so much of his argumentation does not come directly from Scripture. This is not a criticism; in fact, I believe that to be the right approach for developing political theory. The struggle is that VanDrunen attempts to show how his political theory, which has been developed through a natural law study, fits with Scripture. In all fairness, all he needs to do is demonstrate that it does not contradict Scripture but follows along with the general principles it describes. At points, however, one is left feeling as though the implications of biblical passages addressing politics and government are stretched beyond what they actually intend to say. In particular, I was not convinced that Scripture actively teaches a polycentric approach to law (which is not to say that I see it as teaching a monocentric view of law instead). Further, it seemed that more work was needed to show that authority lies in laws and not in government itself, especially given the way that many scriptural exhortations to submit to governing authorities lack any nuance about submitting to them for the sake of the just laws that have arisen from the customs of the people.

Those critiques being stated, the overall impression of this book is quite positive. VanDrunen has helped me to think through some challenging issues in ways I had not before. I have profited from my time in this book. It is recommended to all Christians who are interested in thinking through a God-honoring understanding of politics and government. It may seem to approach these issues in a different way than expected, but I would encourage the reader to give a careful consideration of the approach VanDrunen takes. In particular, using the Noahic covenant as the starting point for developing a political theory is the great strength of this book, and I hope it will have a lasting impact on the development of political theory among Christians.

Printed in Poland
by Amazon Fulfillment
Poland Sp. z o.o., Wrocław

22742044R00074